Evexiandros

The Wellness Philosophy

Spiritual Health Balance Handbook

Emmanuil Ioannis Misodoulakis

GW00472021

Copyright:

Table of Contents:

About the Author:

My name is Mano. I'm an author, blogger, and documentary filmmaker, but besides that, I'm a Natural medicine researcher. My real passion is the search for wellness. Health is everything and knowledge of health, is the most important for everyone. I travel around the world and I explore traditional medicine secrets, alternative treatments, folk healing practices, superfoods, physical activities for well-being, meditation techniques, and philosophy pathways. My real name is Emmanuil, but my author's pen ancient Greek name is **Evexiandros**. I change it, as according to the Ancient Greeks, names should be created by the way you lived your life. Evexiandros (Ευεξιανδρος) is derived from two Greek words: Ευεξια – Evexia that means wellness and Ανδρας that means men. So, my pen name means Men of Wellness, similar to my website: (www.thewellnessseeker.com).

DEDICATED TO ANCIENT GREEK PHILOSOPHERS - THE SOUL DOCTORS.

About this Book:

The Philosophy of Wellness:
Mind-Body-Soul Balance…

Wellness is a state of physical, mental, and spiritual balance and is the only path to bliss. Many thinkers throughout history had spoken about the importance of wellness and balance, but they couldn't solve the riddle. Hippocrates once said that if you are a doctor and philosopher, you are almost a god. With this book, you will understand how important Philosophy is for our health. Philosophy is the best cure for the mind and soul. People without philosophy are unbalanced. Unbalance can cause mental and physical symptoms which can lead to disease. In this journey, you will discover the meditation practices of Pythagoras, Socrates, and the Stoics. The Aristotelian Golden Mean, the sacred Tetractys, and the Pentagram of Pythagoras. You will learn from the demi-god healer Asclepius, about the Snake, and dream Therapies.

Philosophy as Medicine.
Ancient Greek Meditation Secrets.
Greek Medicine.
Philosophy as Psychotherapy.
Spiritual Enlightenment.

We will also explore how Platonism, Cynicism, the Epicurean, and Stoic philosophy can be used as psychotherapy in modern psychology and rediscover the missing link between Christianity and Greek Philosophy. Next, we will investigate the secrets of Apollonius of Tyana, one of the greatest healers of all time. Finally, we shall study why a meat-based diet is not the ideal choice for human health from Plutarch and the Pythagoreans. If you follow the wellness philosophy book everything in your life will improve. Morality is one of the greatest forms of well-being and Philosophy is the medicine of the soul.

Introduction:

As the ancient Roman poet, Publius Vergilius Maro (Virgil) once said, the greatest wealth of life is health. Look around you, it's all about health and wellness. We go to the cinema to watch a movie because it's entertaining, and that's a form of wellness, we listen to music or dance at the nightclubs because it feels good and that's a form of wellness. Even for bad habits like smoking, people who smoke, are getting the benefit of relaxation and pleasure. In a way, they think that smoking is good for them, even if in reality it is killing them. It is in our genes to look for well-being. For example, when we look for a sex partner, we try to find someone who is healthy, strong, and beautiful, with dense nice hair, tight skin, and fit and that's because, in reality, we try to perpetuate our species.

We all have different goals, but in the end, it's all about wellness. The ultimate goal of life and humans is bliss. Some people think that sex is the biggest pleasure, while others prefer food or alcohol, and the list goes on and on… But what is a pleasure, and what has to do with wellness? When does pleasure improve our lives, and when is it merely harming us? These and many more will be analyzed in this book.

The Wellness Philosophy:
and the Bliss (Nirvana) Puzzle:

It's all about perfection and Eudaimonia (Bliss) or as it is called in Buddhism NIRVANA. In my Philosophy, wellness is a state of physical, mental, and spiritual balance. Balanced-well-being is the path to eudaimonia. Some of the ways to achieve this wellness-balance are by practicing the Eastern philosophy of the Middle Path of Taoism and Buddhism religions or by the Aristotelian philosophy of the Golden Mean, (the desirable middle between two extremes). The entire Ancient Philosophy, "particularly the Greek, Hindu, and Chinese," is a continuous process. These philosophies may have controversial topics at times, but this is a good thing because it aids in philosophical development. I attempt to integrate all of these philosophical ideas into a single philosophy, the philosophy of wellness. The underlying motivation behind all of these philosophical notions, in my perspective, is wellness which leads to blis. Wellness is the key to finding balance and can aid in soul evolution. But first, we need to understand what is the Aristotelean golden mean. According to Aristotle, courage would be the golden mean "balance" between recklessness and cowardice. Here are some other examples, kindness is the golden mean between rudeness and flatterers. Power is the golden mean between weakness and exhaustion (extreme physical or mental fatigue). Intelligence is the golden mean between stupidity and paranoia. Some bad habits and emotions such as restlessness, hatred, sadness, avarice, and jealousy can poison our health. In short periods these feelings are completely normal and even healthy, but if we do not balance our negativity it can cause mental and physical symptoms which can lead to disease. Now, let's investigate another Greek term the "MIDEN AGAN" (MHΔEN AΓAN) which means NOTHING IN EXCESS... With the term MIDEN AGAN (nothing in excess) we understand that even negative emotions (for example jealousy) are healthy at the right time. We need to find the golden mean within ourselves and the golden mean in the things and situations in that we are involved. For example, I'm feeling cold today and the weather is cold so I need a hot beverage, if I get a cold beverage instant, I will be freezing and I will be even more out of balance. We need to practice and try to make the Golden Mean our nature, or in other words, we need to be one with our nature. In the Greek language, the word Ευεξία- Evexia (wellness) starts with the prefix "EU" which in ancient Greek means "well or good" and the word "EΞIΣ=EXΩ" which in ancient Greek means to own - to have. So, wellness in Greek means good-being "well-being". If we follow the golden mean (middle path) we will achieve wellness and perfection and as a result, we will achieve bliss (eudaimonia). Many people lecture about the value of moderation and the middle path but they don't completely understand it. The goal is to find the link between our inner and outer limits. A lemon, for example, can be acidic if consumed in excess, but you need to find also your limits of acidity, in order to realize how much lemon will harm you. Another example will be the light of your phone. When set on automatic, your phone looking the average lighting for balance. During the day, will be low as it's more light outside and at night will be higher as it's getting darker. In the Greek language, the "EU" prefix is always used before every good word, like Eutuxia "which means happiness" or eu-poria "prosperity". The prefix "EU" has two letters, the letter E which comes from the word ελλειψη - ellipsis (lack of), and the letter U which comes from the word υπερβολη - Ipervoli (exaggeration)... So, in summary, the Greek "EU" means middle or balance. The balance between Lack and Excess. When you visit the Temple of Apollo in Delphi you will find some of the most important commandments of the Ancient Greek world. Three of the best are, "ΓΝΩΘΙ ΣΑΥΤΟΝ" - KNOW THYSELF, which means, THE KNOWLEDGE IS INSIDE YOU. "ΜΗΔΕΝ ΑΓΑΝ" - NOTHING IN EXCESS" and "ΜΕΤΡΟΝ ΆΡΙΣΤΟΝ - "MODERATION IS BEST". Pythagoras believed that the universe is composed of opposite qualities and that we must stay in balance with these opposite qualities, as it is very important for our health. For Pythagoreans, the ancient Greek word Υγίεια, (today Υγεια, which means health) was the harmony between spirit, body, and soul. Health is represented by the five elements of nature: Air, Fire, Water, Earth, and Aether. As I mentioned before, Pythagoreans believed that Moderation is best. For example, if you eat more than usual, you will feel sick, and if you eat less, you will feel weak. So again, Elipsis "lack of" and Ypervoli "exaggeration" are the root causes of all sickness.

But what About the Extremes?

So, what about the extremes, are they really so bad? No, extremes are necessary and we need them, but even in extremes, there is a balance and a middle path. We need to find balance in extremes. In this picture, you can see a fisherman trying to catch a fish, but he does something extreme because the fish is trying to escape, at the same time he keeps his balance. Extremes force our bodies to adapt and become stronger. If we have control over extremes, our levels of balance rise.

Also, when the body experiences something intense or shocking, it forces mindfulness. A great example is fasting, the more we fast, the more we balance hunger. A person's ability to maintain self-control increases as they consume less.

The Difference Between Pleasure and Wellness:

First of all, I must admit that Epicurus is one of my favorite philosophers and that he was the only philosopher who was so close to my ideas, "as I found out afterwards." Hedonism for Epicurus was the tool for bliss, but for me, there is a big difference between pleasure and well-being. Pleasure could also be a bad thing. Moderate pleasure, on the other hand, is a path to well-being and well-being is the key to eudaimonia. Epicurus, of course, spoke about moderate pleasure. The reward system of the brain is proof that we feel pleasure every time we do something good. Dopamine is a neurotransmitter that is activated when something good happens. Epicurus advised us to rely on our senses, I will agree with him in part, but not entirely, as we now know that our senses can be deceiving. An example is our eyes, the sense of sight has many limitations, but with advances in physics and technology, we can see more things. Now, the truth is that we built this technology with our senses, so somehow Epicurus was right. Another mistake for me in Epicurean philosophy is that pain is something bad. For me this is wrong. Pain is there for a reason. When we exercise, we feel pain, but we gain muscle. Pain from exercise can be a pleasant thing and a result of wellness. Let's look at the sauna as another example. Although the heat in the sauna may make us feel uncomfortable, that doesn't mean there won't be a pleasure and a subsequent feeling of wellness.

Fever, pain, and many other uncomfortable signals or symptoms help our body to recover from illness and get better. That's why moderation and balance are the keys to wellness. In terms of nutrition, Epicurus was right, only a few people eat to improve health and to feel better, and most people out there have linked food with their emotional gaps. A person who is overweight and constantly eats will not experience the true joy of food. A person who is hungry for 20 minutes won't enjoy food as much as someone who is hungry for hours. The more you starve, the greater your pleasure when you finally eat.

Eudaimonia and the Divine:

The Secret for Eternity and Longevity:

The drama of our time is the separation between Science and Philosophy. Science today acts without virtue, ethics, and spiritual values. According to my theory, The Divine is something we can't understand completely, (Not like Neo-Platonism, in which we don't understand the concept of the Divine at all). The Divine cannot be defined but can be known. It is all and nothing, whole but empty, one and many. That's why I'm always laughing when I see people fighting about the existence of God. Atheist, agnostic, or theist they are all right, as the Divine, it's all and nothing. Similar to the Yin Yang theory, the universe springs from the Divine, the Divine is in the universe and guides things on their way. The most important in Yin-Yang dualism is not in the contradictory forces but the line between them, which represents balance.

The opposing forces are united by harmony, as they are interrelated and mutually dependent on each other. And while fate exists, we can change our destiny by karma. If we want to be truly healthy, we must first achieve Mind-Body-Soul balance. As the Roman poet Decimus Iunius Iuvenalis (Juvenal) once said, A Healthy Mind in a Healthy Body (Sit Mens Sana In Corpore Sano). Ayurveda the ancient Indian medicine approaches wellness, by promoting a holistic harmony of the body, mind, and spirit. Like Ancient Greek medicine, Ayurveda focuses on the five elements, Earth, Water, Fire, Air, and Ether. In my wellness philosophy, the ultimate goal of our existence is the perfection of our divine self and the only way to achieve bliss (eudaimonia) is by the middle path.

Now, I need to carry on from where all of our ancient philosophers left us. I attempt to piece together this ancient secret puzzle, as much of this knowledge has been lost. But I'm sure that all of this knowledge is still within us, passed down from generation to generation, and encoded in our DNA. With the evolution of species, the Divine has preserved the knowledge inside us. Socrates believed that our soul is immortal. He also said that death is not the end of our existence. According to Plato, the soul comprises three parts, the rational, the appetitive, and the spirited. The rational soul is the highest part of the soul that seeks the truth. Plato believed that our soul is continually reborn in subsequent bodies. However, Aristotle believed that only one part of the soul was immortal (probably the same rational part of the soul of Plato). Aristotle referred to this as the intellect (ποιητικος νους - logos) and is the part that connects our inner consciousness and soul with the cosmic soul. For Socrates and the Stoics, this highest part of the soul was an inner Demon (spirit), known as "Demonio" in Greek. Jim Morrison's Epitaph has a gravestone with a Greek inscription reading "KATA TON DAIMONA EAYTOY", which literally means, "According to his own Demon". Socrates claimed that was guided by his daemon and he believed was a gift from the gods. As previously stated, the only way to achieve eudaimonia is through the wellness "middle path." We can find small wellness connections with the Divine in our daily life. With balanced art creations, balanced exercise, balanced entertainment, balanced sex, and so on... You will need to lead a moral life and engage in more spiritual pursuits like philosophy and meditation if you want to maintain a long-lasting connection with eudaimonia. The more we connect with the Divine through the inner highest part of our soul, the more likely it is that we will achieve eudaimonia after death as a final step of perfection, and break the endless cycle of reincarnation. The inner highest part of the soul is like duplicating Carbon that copies our experiences for an exam.

Aether the Life Force:

As I mentioned before for Pythagoras health (Υγεια) is represented by the five elements of nature, Air, Fire, Water, Earth, and Aether. Water, according to Thales of Miletus, is the originating principle. Anaximenes of Miletus held that air was the primary substance in all things. The fire, according to Heraclitus of Ephesus, was the beginning of everything.

Another theory comes from Anaximander that believed that neither of the so-called elements, is the originating principle, but a different substance, the Infinite [ἄπειρον]. In my opinion, Anaximander was one of the best philosophers of the pre-Socratic period. The air of Anaximenes was constantly in motion, just like the infinite of Anaximander. Finally, Aristotle said that Aether is the essence and spirit of the other four elements. Timaeus, by Plato, has an accurate and symbolic description of how Aether produces life. Aether according to Hesiod's Theogony was a deity born from the union of Night and Erebus. Orphism was considered Aether as the soul of the world. In quantum physics, a new era of Aether-fans begins, which supported the convergence of physics and metaphysics. Today, Aether's theorists believe that this energy is a spiral foundation of the universe, which cannot be measured by instruments because it moves very fast and this is why our Universe is filled with spirals from galaxies to electrons.

In 1905 Einstein rejected the Aether theory, but in 1920 Albert Einstein stated: "According to the general theory of relativity <u>space without Aether is unthinkable.</u> For in such space there not only would be no propagation of light, but also no possibility of existence for standards of space and time… Many cultures share the same principles. Aether, Chi, Reiki, Prana, Orgone, or Life Force are all synonyms for the same power.

Chi:

For the Chinese, Chi is the energy process of the dynamic balancing of Yin and Yang, the electromagnetic energy that flows through everything in the Universe. Tai chi, the ancient Taoist martial art is promoting health and longevity.

Prana:

Aether is the so-called prana of Indian philosophy, which permeates all of Creation. Prana is a Sanskrit word meaning "life-force". It is an invisible bio-vital energy that keeps the body alive.

Orgone:

Wilhelm Reich, an Austrian doctor, and psychoanalyst "discovered" orgone, an idea of primary cosmic energy found everywhere in the universe. Reich had a theory that an orgasm can generate large quantities of a special form of energy called orgone. A similar idea to the Kundalini-prana energy of ancient India.

Reiki:

The Japanese Reiki is a spiritual healing practice, that is known as palm healing. It is useful for the treatment of physical and mental trauma and supports well-being.

Spiral the Symbol of Nature:

The spiral is everywhere in the universe, in the turbulence of rivers or gas, in plants, and even in DNA! Dating back at least to the Neolithic period. Why does it have so much positive meaning for every culture? You can find the spiral symbol in the art of every culture around the world. Man is on a journey we don't know where we come from or where we may be going. As I have stated, it's possible that certain ancient secrets are preserved in our DNA from generation to generation.

The Caduceus is a 6,000-year-old ancient Symbol. It's a helix "a three-dimensional spiral". The Caduceus of Hermes is a Medical Symbol, and it is so interesting how similar it is to the Double Helix of our DNA. As I said above theorists of Aether believe that Aether is a spiral foundation of the universe. Also, spirals are common in Orgonites for directing the energy flow. In Chen's style of Tai Chi, the Yin Yang symbol is replaced by a spiral symbol. Spiraling energy exercises are one of the fundamentals of Chen Taiji.

Several cultures, including those of Africa, Ancient Greece, Malta, the Inca tribe of Peru, and Japan, have used the spiral in their art.

In ancient Britain, the spiral is the symbol of fertility. A perfect example of the spiral symbol is at the gate of supreme harmony in the forbidden city of China. The palace is guarded by two massive bronze lions! The Male lion playing with a spiral ball symbolizes the world, and the female with a cub symbolizes longevity! It's fascinating how certain cultures, which are so significantly different from each other, discovered spiral expressions that are so similar!

The Pythagorean Harmonic Methods of Healing:

Pythagoras of Samos was a great philosopher, mathematician, geometer, and musician. He was a student of Thales of Miletus and he traveled to all known spiritual places of his time for only one reason, knowledge. For him, numbers and mathematics were the essence of life and one with the divine. He said that the earth is round and that we have a heliocentric solar system 2000 years before Copernicus. One of the most famous Pythagoras quotes was, "the art of living happily is to live in present". Therefore in a sense Pythagoras had an influence on the stoic philosophy. The Pythagoreans believed in reincarnation, that the soul is divine and that it occupies a different body after death, human or animal. The student had to adopt a completely different way of life, frequent fasting, abstinence from any animal food, the prohibition of any religious sacrifice, etc... Pythagoras traveled extensively, according to Diogenes Laertius, visiting not only Egypt but also Arabia, Phoenicia, Judaea, Babylon, and even India in his quest to collect all knowledge about the gods and their mystic or hidden cults. His philosophy was influenced by his studies in these countries, as well as by the significance of sacred numbers in the Orphic Mysteries. In the early stages, the Pythagoreans had to remain silent for five years. The Pythagorean student was limited to listening to the teachings without asking for any explanation. Students couldn't meet the teacher, who was hiding behind a curtain.

Pythagoras was the first philosopher that connected astronomy with music, arguing that in the harmonious and comprehensive universe everything is governed by simple laws, which can be expressed with numbers "sacred Tetractys". Pythagoras taught that the four elements constitute a Tetrakty (Tetractys 1+2+3+4=10), corresponding to the fire for the unit, the air for the number two, the water for the number three, and the earth for the number four.

```
          •
        •   •
      •   •   •
    •   •   •   •
```

Mystics like Pythagoras were able to listen to the sacred curative sounds and knew about the Cosmic vibration healing powers. Pythagoras had reached such a level of sensitivity to hear (not with ears) the agreement of the sky, the music of the celestial spheres as he called (The Harmony of the Spheres)! The vibrating and harmonic universe described by quantum physics' String Theory is identical to the vibrating and harmonic universe described by Pythagoras in his cosmogony "The Music of the Spheres," in which the entire cosmos vibrate like a huge musical instrument. Plato defined music as the movement of sound to reach the soul and demonstrate its virtue. As Iamblichus tells us, "On the Pythagorean life, 938 to 958," Pythagoras employed an undefinable divine and mysterious method in order to hear the secrets and music of the universe. Pythagoreans valued music and mathematics above all else. The harmonious relations of numbers transferred to the planets. The phrase "music of the spheres" refers to the intertwined relationship between the structures of music and those of the physical world. Pythagoras' music of the spheres theory comes into existence with Nasa discoveries. NASA took the electromagnetic signals coming from the planets and converted them to human sounds. The most amazing about the sounds of the planets is that strictly related to the seven notes. The correspondences of the seven major planets in music sounds (notes) are:

1) Sun = Mi
2) Venus = Fa
3) Mercury = Sol
4) Moon = La
5) Saturn = Si
6) Mars = Re
7) Jupiter = Do

The Golden ratio Phi, 1.618 or φ = 1.618

The golden ratio Phi, 1.618, or φ = 1.618 in Greek is the ratio of balance. The golden number φ was detected for the first time by the ancient Greeks, who observed that everything on earth, from plants to the human body itself, was based on a harmonious analogy. This harmony is found in many elements of nature and could not go unnoticed by the highly observant ancient Greek mathematicians. Pythagoras spent much time of his life finding this "magic number". Each side is divided into two smaller sections, and if you divide the length of the largest section by the smallest section the ratio will be equal to F (φ). The golden ratio Phi appears in the proportions of the Pentalpha, the secret sign of the Pythagorean School. The Pythagorean Pentalpha symbolizes the healthy balance of the five elements and the rise of Humanity. It is an implicit number, a number that cannot be derived from the product of two others, which has infinite decimal elements. In short, the number is not measurable, but it is approximate. The letter "φ" - Phi, 1.618 symbolizes the Golden mean "Golden Section ratio". Once the Golden Section became known, many artists began to use it, to give a sense of "perfection" in their work. Applications of this "magic" number can be found in architecture, sculpture, painting, and even music.

Pentagram Protection, Perfection, and Balance:

The pentagram first appeared in Mesopotamia, Ancient Greece, and Babylonia. An inverted pentagram is a symbol of evil because it presented an inversion of the natural order. The word Pentagram derives from the Greek pente, "five" and gramma, "letter". The meaning of the inverted Pentagram as a demonic symbol is very recent (from the 19th century). Ancient Greeks used the Pentagram as a microcosm of the human body. Pentagram has been used as a symbol of protection, balance, and perfection in spirituality from the beginning of recorded history. In magic, pentacles were used as a symbol of protection. If something was within the circle of the Pentagram, it was protected from the dark forces. Pythagoreans considered it an emblem of perfection. As I mentioned before the pentacle is associated with the Pythagorean theorem and the golden mean (the desirable middle between two extremes). Also, the pentacle inside the Pentagram forms 10 angles, (Tetractys) 10 for the Pythagoreans was a perfect number.

The Pythagorean, Alcmaeon of Croton, taught that health was a harmonious balance of the opposites. The disease is a result that derives from excess and deficiency. Here is an example, excess heat causes fever, and excess cold causes chills (Lois N. Magner). Pentacle will protect the seeker from all Evil influences. It is spiritual, physical, and mental protection against evil. Evil can't pass where Pentacle is displayed. In Reiki, Pentagram is placed into the solar plexus, heart, and root chakra for healing and protection. Wearing a Pentagram symbolizes one's connection to Mother Earth and all of nature's elements.

Pythagorean Meditation:

What many people do not know about Pythagoras is that he was also a healer. Throughout his travels to Egypt and even India, Pythagoras gained a great deal of knowledge about meditation. He fasted for 40 days prior to his exams at the renowned Alexandria School.

"So you will have to go on a 40 day fast, continuously breathing in a certain manner (Pranayama)*, with a certain awareness on certain points* (Chakras)."

According to Porphyry, Pythagoras advised his students to meditate twice a day, once when they got out of bed and once before going to sleep. The following words were the basis for the daily personal Moral self-purification of every Pythagorean just before going to bed. This methodology brought the student face to face with himself:

«Πῆι παρέβην; - Τί δ' ἔρεξα; - Τί μοι δέον οὐκ ἐτελέσθη;»

"What did I do that I shouldn't? What did I do right? What should I have done and I didn't?"

The Pythagorean Meditation is so beneficial for health that researchers at the University of Athens have created a new technique, called "Pythagorean self-awareness for stress management, memory improvement, and wellness". The research aims to contribute to the reduction of stress and the improvement of memory. In a series of experiments performed on patients with Mild Cognitive Disorder, Pythagorean Meditation improved mental performance, memory, attention, and perception.

The Ancient Greek Medicine
(Unani medicine)

We all know that Greece is the foundation of Western civilization. The history of Greece is huge and in the times of Great Alexander Hellenism spread from Anatolia, Syria, Judea, Phoenicia, Gaza, Mesopotamia, Egypt, and Persia, until India. Ancient Greek medicine together with the Egyptian and the Chinese were the most important Medicines of the Ancient world. Greeks are considered by many the founders of Western medicine. From Asclepius to Hippocrates and Galen, Greek medicine is around 4000 years old. Today we have evidence and DNA analysis about the medical pills found aboard an ancient Greek ship. Natural substances like alfalfa, carrot, celery, radish, oak, wild onion, cabbage, and yarrow were found inside these pills. These pills are evidence of ancient Greek medicine with an incredible network and an international trade from ancient times.

Unani Medicine:

Another piece of evidence of how important Ancient Greek medicine is, even in our times is the Unani medicine. Practiced in Middle-East, Central, and South-Asian countries, and especially India. This Perso-Arabic system was found in the doctrines of the ancient Greek physicians, Hippocrates and Galen, and was re-discovered with the help of Persian physicians, such as Avicenna (Abu Ali Sina), Rhazes (al-Razi), Al Zahrawi, and Ibn Nafis. Unani in the Arabic language means ("Ionian"/"Greek"). The balance of the four humors - lood, phlegm, yellow bile, and black bile - which are body fluids - is crucial to unani medicine. Environmental conditions can also significantly affect health. Like in Ayurveda and Chinese medicine, in Unani medicine diseases comes from the imbalance of the four elements, air, fire, water, and earth. It is a philosophical medical system that it's based on today's scientific evidence and diagnosis mixed up with the natural holistic principles of healing.

Hygieia the Goddess of Health:

For me, she is symbolizing one of the most important archetypes (health above all). Her name appears for the first time in the Homeric epics. At first, was only the personification of an abstract idea. As a result, it had no distinct personality and was used to refer to other deities, particularly Athena. She evolved into a specific goddess over time, and when she was finally identified as Asclepius' daughter, she was given the same symbol, a snake. However, while Asclepius is directly associated with the treatment of diseases, the goddess was associated with the prevention of diseases and the maintenance of a state of health. In short, Asclepius represents healing, while the goddess represents prevention and a perfect state of health. Her sisters were Panakeia (Panacea) (Cure-All) and Iaso (Remedy). The Nosoi were Hygeia's enemies (Spirits of Disease).

Asclepius:

Asclepius was a demi-god healer and a god of medicine. Was so powerful, that he was able to heal all humans. Was the Son of the God Apollo and the mortal Thessalian princess Coronis. Asclepius temples were hospital-temples with a clean environment. The Greek God of medicine was named Vediovis in Roman and Etruscan mythology. The rod of Asclepius remains a symbol of medicine today. Was Asclepius a real person? Asclepius was originally a mortal, but later, because of his healing abilities, he became the God of medicine. In ancient times people from all over Europe visited Asclepius to receive his wisdom and healing powers.

Asclepius Snake Therapy:

It is said that Asclepius arrived once, in his temples of worship, transformed into a snake. The Asklepios name has not yet been interpreted, but it is likely to be associated with snakes. In the Greek language "Aσκλ" is produced by Ασκάλαβο, meaning snake, lizard, reptile. In many myths of Asclepius, a snake kisses the patient, and then the patient is healed. Here is an excerpt from Greek mythology: A patient, with a bad wound on his toe, was moved by Asclepius's assistants into the temple and then slept. Sleeping while awake, the patient saw the sacred snake coming out from a sacred place and licking his wound. After an hour he woke up healthy. Today science can give us more clues about how snake venom can be used as an 'alternative' medicine for many diseases. Modern research supports the idea that snake poison neurotoxins and hemotoxins may have a lot of health benefits and can be used to create drugs that can treat heart disease, Alzheimer's, and memory loss. So how did the ancient Greeks adjust the venom in the first place?

Amazingly they may have drunk it. Evidence has shown that the Ancient Greeks may have discovered the healing powers of snake venom long before we did!

Asclepius Dream Healing:

Ancient Greeks placed a high value to sleep, and that's due to the mystical and healing effects of dreams. Sleep therapy was practiced often in Asclepius treatment centers. It was a ritual practice. The patient had to sleep in a sacred place to receive a revealing dream for therapeutic purposes. After a physical and mental cleansing process, the patient must sleep in the sacred place and seek a revealing dream, a contact with the Divine inside the dream for healing recovery. In preparation, were other parts like special diets, fasting, bathing, musical events, inhaling fumes (probably psychotropic substances), and conversations with the monks and the doctors of Asklepios. Patients drank tea from herbs and other therapeutic mixtures and indeed, as mentioned, most of the time, the sick was feeling better with this process. After the herbal teas, the patient had to stand in the sacred fountain. The water of the fountain was used for body cleansing and psychic purification. Religious ceremonies strengthen patients' faith in order to approach the Divine.

Hippocrates:

Hippocrates was a Greek philosopher and physician that born around 460 BC on the island of Kos. He is widely known as the father of modern medicine. Sleep, diet, mental stress, and exercise are all important factors for patients' treatment. He was the first that rejected the views of his time that illness was caused by evil spirits and the gods. Hippocrates said that if you are a doctor and philosopher you are almost a god. The reputation of Hippocrates was huge and influenced all subsequent philosophers and doctors. Many new doctors were really surprised when they first read, that 24 centuries ago Hippocratic doctors knew almost all of our today's diseases. That's also one of the reasons that so many medical terms are derived from the Greek language! Hippocrates had his school in Kos and wrote 59 books. In general, ancient Greeks usually died at old age, if we exclude deaths from wars and epidemics. Hippocrates knew all about anatomy. He also invented special surgical instruments and proceeded with difficult surgeries. He disinfected surgical instruments every time before surgery, with fire or inside old wine (rich in alcohol).

Few people know that Hippocrates also founded homeopathy. He had a famous quote about homeopathy: «τα όμοια των ομοίων εισίν ιάματα», which means: the same can be treated with the same. Hippocrates and other doctors of ancient Greece likely used homeopathic medicines, like potent drugs diluted to such an extent that is not toxic but can cause symptoms similar to the disease.

Hippocrates Treatments:

The theory of the four body juices was formulated and disseminated by some students of Hippocrates and was based on the theory of the four elements of Empedocles. Hippocrates said that the juices of the body may vary according to the seasons. In Winter phlegm increases due to cold. In Spring phlegm still prevails, but the blood begins to strengthen. Because the days are getting warmer in Summer, blood predominates, while the bile becomes stronger in Autumn. Hippocrates centuries ago, suggested immersion in hot or cold water for the treatment of various diseases such as muscular spasms, paralysis, rheumatism, and arthropathies.

The Hippocrates Diet:

Hippocrates said: We are what we eat. The Hippocratic diet is based on the balance of the five basic human tastes. The bitter, the salty, the sweet, the sour, and the astringent. These components when mixed and combined, are not affecting negatively humans. But when some of them are separated and used alone for a long period can cause imbalance and diseases.

For example, people that are addicted to sugar or salt and don't eat bitter or sour food can cause immune system illness.

When Hippocrates Met Socrates During the Deadly Plague of Athens:

In the years of the painful Peloponnesian civil war, in 430 BC, Hippocrates, the "father of medicine," faced the most terrible epidemic that struck the city of Athens, the terrible and deadly plague of ancient Greece. The plague was spread by an Egyptian ship to Athens, which was under siege by the Spartans. The majority of the population was infected, and up to 75,000 people died. Thucydides, the renowned historian who was younger at the time of the epidemic, experienced the plague firsthand, fell ill, survived, and meticulously chronicled his symptoms. Litanies and incense offerings by the priests were desperate attempts to prevent the doom of the city. Pericles called the renowned Hippocrates from Kos to control the plague. In three months, Hippocrates was able to put an end to the plague. Socrates and Hippocrates met during the pandemic and had lengthy conversations. They had something in common, while the one tried to heal the souls, the second cured the bodies. Hippocrates discovered the cure for the plague after observing that blacksmiths were not offended. As a result, He realized that fire was protecting them. So he gave the order to burn the infected clothes, mattresses, and anything else touched by the sick. He also observed that anyone living near water wells was contaminated. As a result, he ordered clean water to be brought from the island of Aegina every day. Athens rewarded the great Doctor with a golden crown, as well as honorary lifelong feeding in the Rectory and initiation into the Eleusinian Mysteries. Unfortunately, the plague killed Pericles, his renowned wife Aspasia, and their two children.

Hippocratic Oath:

The Hippocratic Oath is one of the oldest binding documents in history, an oath that is taken by all physicians.

Hippocrates Best Quotes:

Make a habit of two things: to help or at least to do no harm.

Let food be the medicine and medicine be the food.

Natural forces within us are the true healers of disease.

A wise man should consider that health is the greatest of human blessings.

Walking is man's best medicine.

It is more important to know what sort of person has a disease than to know what sort of disease a person has.

What medicines do not heal, the lance will, what the lance does not heal, the fire will.

Galen:

The Greek Galen (Galēnos, 129–c. 200 CE) of Pergamon was the best physician of ancient Rome in the time of Marcus Aurelius. His books and works still survive with about 20,000 pages. He is famous for his anatomical and surgery discoveries. Galen was also a Philosopher, (believed in the Aristotelian doctrine) and he mixed his philosophy into his medicine. For sure, he was the most important physician in the ancient world after Hippocrates.

Dioscorides:

Dioscorides was one of the best physicians, pharmacologists, and herbalists of the Ancient World. Was born in the Anazarbo of Cilicia in 40 AD. Dioscorides was traveling as a surgeon with the armies of the Roman emperor Nero. During his journey, He researched the medicinal properties of numerous herbs, plants, and minerals. Later on, Dioscorides published the De Materia Medica, "On Medicinal Substances" in five volumes. De Materia Medica describes the properties of over one thousand medicinal substances.

Other Famous Physicians from Greece:

Herophilus, Erasistratus, Asclepiades of Bithynia, Soranus of Ephesus, Menodotus of Nicomedia, Diocles of Carystus, Praxagoras, Apollonios of Kition, Alexander of Tralles, Philistion of Locri, Rufus of Ephesus, Philinus of Cos, Athenaeus of Attalia, Demosthenes Philalethes, Philonides, Aspasia the Physician, Hicesius, Antiphanes of Delos, Alcmaeon of Croton, Philip of Acarnania, Aretaeus of Cappadocia, Democedes, and Herodicus.

Socrates the Physician of the Soul and his Legacy to the World:

Socrates is the father of philosophy. My research for wellness will be incomplete without a chapter about Socrates. For me the assumption that Socrates is the greatest philosopher of all times is unquestionable. He was so important that Greek philosophy is divided into the period before Socrates and after. His life and death are considered an example to follow for the next generation of philosophers. Socrates was born in Athens in 469 BC. His father was the stonemason Sophroniskos, and his mother was the midwife Fainareti. At the age of 17, he met the philosopher Archelaus and he starts to consider that philosophy is a divine command. It is this divine command that makes him a great philosopher in the sense of doing what was right and avoiding what is not. This Virtue is what Socrates calls daemon «δαιμόνιο». He spent his life in the markets and streets of Athens and his teachings influenced almost all philosophical schools after him. Unlike Sophists, he did not take money from his students. He married Xanthippe, a devoted wife, and mother at an old age and they had three children. Xanthippe was much younger than him and an extremely dynamic woman. Sometimes she was aggressive and violent against him. Socrates agreed that Xanthippi was wild. He said that he chose her precisely because of her argumentative spirit.

Once said: "*It is like a rider who wishes to become an expert horseman. I know full well, if I can tolerate her spirit, I can with ease attach myself to every human being else.*"

I believe Xanthippi was also the inspiration for this amusing Socratic marriage quote:

"*My advice to you is to get married: if you find a good wife, you'll be happy if not, you'll become a philosopher.*"

Socratic Discipline as Medicine:

According to Socrates, fewer needs lead to greater abundance. Those who have fewer needs are considered truly wealthy.

"*He who is not contented with what he has, would not be contented with what he would like to have.*"

"*The secret of happiness, you see, is not found in seeking more, but in developing the capacity to enjoy less.*"

In 430 BC, Athens was devastated by the plague, which killed approximately one-third of the population, including the Greek statesman Pericles. Socrates was not just a Philosopher but also a "super-human". During these difficult times when the Athenians were dying from plague and starving for food, Socrates practiced frugality and fasted without any problem. He was claiming that the fewer needs a man has, the closer he is to the gods.

"Socrates was so well-disciplined in his way of life that on several occasions when plague broke out in Athens, he was the only man who escaped infection. " — **Diogenes Laertius**.

Socrates was neither rich nor aristocratic, but well-known names of the Athenian aristocracy, such as Alcibiades, Harmidis and Kritias, belonged to the close circle of his students.

The Philosophy of Socrates:

He is the first philosopher who deals systematically with ethics. He is dedicated, to the cultivation of the soul and constant self-control. With Socrates, philosophy turns to a study of human behavior and becomes anthropocentric. Self-awareness is the purpose of Socrates.

In his philosophical discussions, which were based on live dialogue, Socrates pretended that he did not know but was interested in learning. The pretense of ignorance is called Socratic irony. He was trying to provoke his interlocutor with questions to discover the knowledge he had inside him, «Γνῶθι σαυτόν = Know thyself = knowledge is inside you». This method is called the obstetric of Socrates, because, like his mother, during her work as a midwife, she delivered a newborn baby, Socrates delivered the truth from his interlocutor. His technique is still used today, mainly in law schools. However, it is also used at Broadmoor Psychiatric Hospital in the South of England since the 1990s. Socrates refers to himself as a gadfly, because he bites the complacent citizens and wakes them from lethargy. According to a Delphic oracle, Socrates was considered the wisest of all men. Socrates was surprised to learn this because he believed he was not wise at all. On the other hand, he could not believe that gods would ever lie. So, what was happening? Was Socrates the wisest of men or not? To solve this question, Socrates decided to visit some famous wise people and ask them questions. Surprised, however, he found that they were not wise. When he tried to express his reservations about their knowledge, they became angry with him. In the end, he concluded that the fact that he was aware of his ignorance, made the Gods decide that Socrates was the wisest of all men. The soul plays a central role in the philosophy of Socrates. He encouraged people to come into contact with their souls. The soul for Socrates was the immortal part of humans and Ethics was the best medicine for the soul.

Socrates said, *"It is better to suffer injustice than to commit it"*. Socrates believed that we do wrong out of ignorance. Evil is a result of ignorance. We always choose what we think is good for us, but many times we choose wrong out of ignorance.

Socratic Meditation and Pythagoreanism:

Socrates used many times Pythagorean and Orphic Myths and allegories. The Pythagorean influence on Plato derives from Socrates. When Socrates spoke about the Pythagoreans he referred to them as these wise men. Two main influences (teachers) of Socrates were Parmenides and Diotima of Mantinea. Parmenides studied with Pythagoreans and Diotima was a priestess of Apollo and a mystic of the Pythagorean numerology. We already know that the Stoics practiced a type of meditation that they learned from the Pythagoreans, but what about Socrates? According to **Ion of Chios**, in his youth, Socrates traveled to Samos and purchased Pythagoras' books. When Samos rebelled against Athens, Pericles and Socrates went into battle and won, taking all of the Samian warships with them. Socrates left the island with two urns full of Pythagorean papyri, which a kind relative had agreed to sell him. It took months to read them, and during that time, Socrates was fascinated by Pythagoras' expanding worldview. After months of study, Socrates kept from Pythagoras the advice to "practice" every day in order to strengthen and develop an iron will. A challenging mind exercise that lasted for a long time.

He strengthened his will and subdued all the wild desires of his mortal nature by living as a hermit. Crito, Socrates' childhood friend, became concerned after not seeing him for several weeks and went to his father's house. He found the house in disarray when he entered it. As he approached the bedroom, he noticed Socrates sitting still in front of the open window and despite the fact that Socrates appeared distant, he had a strange sense of bliss.

Crito asked him what his up to and why he was sitting still. Socrates answered:

"Im Practicing. I train my soul."

Crito —"To fight against whom?"

Socrates — "One of my biggest enemies, myself."

In Plato's Symposium, there are two accounts of instances in which Socrates meditates. Another reference to meditation is found in Phaedo. Alcibiades mentions how Socrates meditated for a whole day and it's clear that he was not praying, but meditating.

Plat. Sym. 220c

Alcibiades tells the dinner guests of another such time Socrates stood, but this was not a short venture as the one of early this evening. At Potidaea, in the Peloponnesian War, Socrates "*joined his thoughts with himself*" and stood still from the morning, through lunch and the evening, and all through the night until the next morning. Alcibiades states that we would not give up, suggesting a commitment to the process despite outside pressures. It was such a sight, that others brought their bedrolls outside to watch. In the morning, he greeted the sun with prayers for the new day.

Plat. Sym. 174d – 175c

Socrates invites his friend Aristodemus to a dinner which is hosted by Agathon. Along the way, Socrates begins to lag behind, and he waves his friend onward. Upon arriving at the house, he takes up a post on the neighbor's porch and stands meditating. Aristodemus enters the house, and Agathon asks where Socrates is and sends a servant to collect the man. When asked by the servant to come in, he refuses. When the servant reports the happening, Agathon orders him to continue to pester Socrates until he comes in, at which point Aristodemus intervenes and asks the host to let Socrates be, as this is a habit of his which he does frequently, regardless of time and place; and that he will be along shortly.

Plato - Phaedo, section 65c
At this point, in Phaedo, Socrates mentions something important about meditation:

"When does the soul attain to the truth? For when it tries to consider anything in company with the body, it is evidently deceived by it. But it thinks best when none of these things troubles it, neither hearing nor sight, nor pain nor any pleasure, but it is, so far as possible, alone by itself, and takes leave of the body, and avoiding, so far as it can, all association or contact with the body, reaches out toward the reality."

Socrates Last Lesson:

In 399 BC the philosopher is accused by his Athenian opponents that refusing to recognize the gods and corrupting the youth of Athens. During the trial, Socrates showed great courage and said that the best punishment he deserves is to be fed for free forever by the state. From Plato's dialogue, we learn that Socrates could be saved if he wanted to since his friends had the opportunity to help him escape. Socrates refused, and as a true philosopher, he drank the conium as required by law. On his trial, Socrates uses his death to teach us a final lesson. He said:

I do not care about death. All I care about is not doing something unfair. Why should I be afraid of death? No one knows what death is, so how can I fear something I don't know? Perhaps is the greatest good for man, and yet we fear death as it is the greatest evil. But now it is time for us to leave, me to die, and you to live. Which of the two is the best is unknown to us. Only God knows.

I have always thought that to need nothing is divine, and to need as little as possible is the nearest approach to the divine, and that what is divine is best, and what is nearest to the divine is the next best. — *Memorabilia*

Platonism and Redemption:

Plato was Socrates' student and Aristotle was Plato's best student. Aristotle and Plato are generally regarded as the two greatest figures of Western philosophy. Socrates influenced Plato and Plato influenced Aristotle, but the Philosophy of both moved in a different direction, complementing each other.

Plato:

Plato was born in Athens to an aristocratic family. He was the Son of Ariston. At the age of twenty, he met Socrates and abandoned poetry. Socrates never wrote anything, everything we know about him is from the writings of Plato. He traveled to Egypt and Cyrene, where he is associated with many wise people. He also made three trips to Italy and Sicily, where he studied the philosophy of Pythagoras. Later from Archytas of Tarentum, he was initiated into Orphism. Plato's work is deeply influenced by the philosophy of the Pythagoreans. When he returned to Athens in 387 BC, he founded his philosophical school, "the Academy". Aristotle studied there for twenty years before founding his own school.

Platonic Idealism and Soul Healing:

Plato believed that the soul is immortal and that only through the psyche beings can be living. The soul is the driving force behind the body and mind. Plato said: "The body is the temple of the soul". According to the Tripartite Theory of Plato, the soul has three parts: the rational (reason), spirited (desires) and appetitive (emotions) parts. As a result, he also acknowledges three virtues: Wisdom, courage, and prudence, each of which corresponds to one of the three parts of the soul. Plato believed these three elements of the psyche should be in balance. Through the harmonious development of those three parts comes justice, which is the balance of the other three virtues and which somehow coordinates and supervises the other three virtues' tasks. The core of the Platonic theory of Ideas is that in addition to the ever-changing perceptible reality, there are some self-existent, unchanging, and imaginary entities, the "Ideas". Objects of the perceptible world owe their existence and any truth to their relationship with Ideas. In Plato's theory, Plato supports his overall interpretation of reality. I will give an example of a river.

The river is never the same as it always changes and we have many rivers, but the idea of the river is always the same. When we say river, we always mean a place with a natural flowing watercourse that begins on hills, high ground, or mountains and flows downwards until it reaches the sea. So, the idea of the river is unchangeable. The perceptible world, on the other hand, is constantly changing, without stability. Plato's Ideas have an authentic existence, they are captured by the intellect, and they are eternal, unborn, and incorruptible. All moral values are Ideas: Virtue, justice, courage, wisdom, and so on... In a way, Plato connected the Eleatic philosophy of Parmenides with the Ionian philosophy of Heraclitus. Plato's Idealism is the golden mean between those two philosophies. The perceptible world represents the body and the unchangeable world represents the soul. The Reason "Logic" is the leader and must be in harmony with the two unlogic powers of the soul, "Feelings", and "Desires". Those three powers must connect into one, by the leadership of Reason "Logic". This can be accomplished only if feelings and desires obey logic. The alliance of feelings and desires with logic gives birth to the logic of the heart. In other words, if the mind does not agree with the emotions, and desires, we will become ill, much like the repressed emotions of modern psychology. The Platonic Philosophy doesn't want us to bury our emotions, but to be in harmony with them. Listening to our feelings while not becoming enslaved by them. Platonism does not punish the body like Hinduism.

Is it not also true that no physician, in so far as he is a physician, considers or enjoins what is for the physician's interest, but that all seek the good of their patients For we have agreed that a physician strictly so called, is a ruler of bodies, and not a maker of money, have we not. —Plato

Cynicism, the Harmonical
Philosophy of Nature:

The Cynics were one of the most important Philosophical Schools in antiquity which was founded by Antisthenes (4th BC), a student of Socrates. The "Cynics" were spiritual descendants of Socrates. They were something like ancient hippies and had the dog as their common symbol. That's why they walked barefoot and ate in public places "just like dogs". An important cynic and student of Antisthenes was Diogenes of Sinope. Some scholars agree that could have been the first anarchist in world history.

When Diogenes was asked what he does and they call him a Cynic "dog", he replied: "I scold those who give me. Those who do not give me, I bark, and I bite the bad fellas". The purpose of life for Cynics is to live in virtue, and in agreement with nature. The Cynics revolted peacefully against the bad consequences of the civilization of their time and tried to bring the great universal values back to light. Temperance and discipline were the key features of this philosophy. The immediate purpose was morality and the result the bliss. For them, the virtuous life consists of the victory of man over desires. Christianity was strongly influenced by Cynic philosophy, especially for those who wanted a monastic life. Serious studies on that subject showed that the first Christians were followers of Cynic philosophy! Many of the Cynic philosophers were from wealthy families, but they distributed their fortunes to the poor. Something we also see later in Christianity.

Diogenis Top Quotes:

"Dogs and philosophers do the greatest good and get the fewest rewards."

"We have two ears and one tongue so that we would listen more and talk less."

"Of what use is a philosopher who doesn't hurt anybody's feelings?"

"Alexander the Great found the philosopher looking attentively at a pile of human bones. Diogenes explained, "I am searching for the bones of your father but cannot distinguish them from those of a slave."

"It takes a wise man to discover a wise man."

"A philosopher named Aristippus, who had quite willingly sucked up to Dionysus and won himself a spot at his court, saw Diogenes cooking lentils for a meal. "If you would only learn to compliment Dionysus, you wouldn't have to live on lentils."

Diogenes replied, "But if you would only learn to live on lentils, you wouldn't have to flatter Dionysus."

"When someone reminded him that the people of Sinope had sentenced him to exile, he said, "And I sentenced them to stay at home."

"There is only a finger's difference between a wise man and a fool."

"To one who asked what was the proper time for lunch, he said, "If a rich man, when you will; if a poor man, when you can."

"I know nothing, except the fact of my ignorance."

Aristotelian Golden Mean and Ethical Principles

As I mentioned before Plato was Socrates' student and Aristotle was Plato's best student. Aristotle (384-322 B.C.) was a Greek philosopher who was a polymath, encyclopedist, the founder of rationalism, and the most important dialectician of ancient times. He is so amazing that I feel compelled to dedicate an entire book to him. Here are some topics he investigated: Cosmology, Physics, Rhetoric, Metaphysics, Ethics and Politics, Mathematics Geology, Biology, and Psychology.

Aristotle Early Life:

Aristotle was born in Stagira on the peninsula of Halkidiki. His father Nicomachus was the personal physician of King Amyntas of Macedonia and grandfather of Alexander the Great. As Nicomachus was a doctor, we can easily understand where Aristotle's interest in the natural sciences and especially biology came from. His parents died when he was young, and he was sent to Athens at the age of 17 to study at Plato's school. He spent 20 years as a student and teacher at the Platonic academy. Aristotle was invited by Philip II to become the head of the Macedonian royal academy and tutor of Alexander the Great.

Aristotle Golden Mean:

As I mentioned at the start Aristotle believed that only one part of the soul was immortal (probably the same as Plato's rational part of the soul). That part for Aristotle was called the intellect (ποιητικος νους - logos), and connecting our inner consciousness and soul with the cosmic soul. The philosophy of the Middle Way of Taoism and Buddhism has many similarities with the Aristotelian philosophy of the Golden Mean, (the desirable middle between two extremes). For example, according to Aristotle, courage is the desirable middle between recklessness and cowardice, kindness is the desirable middle between rudeness and flattering, and so on... *"First of all, it must be observed that the nature of moral qualities is such that they are destroyed by defect and by excess. We see the same thing happen in the case of strength and health. Both excessive and defective exercise destroys the strength, and similarly drink or food which is above or below a certain amount destroys the health"*. Nicomachean Ethics 1104a. Virtue cannot exist unless it is based on the golden middle path.

To put it another way, there is no middle path that does not lead to virtue. And of course, Golden mean should not be confused with mediocrity. Unfortunately, English is not the best language for describing the Golden Mean. Mediocrity refers to the point between the excellent and the bad, while the Golden mean has to do only with the excellent. The middle way is suggested as a balance that neutralizes the risks of both ends. In ethics, because the balance in behavior is only one point, in contrast to the infinities of ends, finding and achieving the middle path is a difficult thing: The mistake can be done in many ways. About life extremes, Aristotle used to say that you can go to extremes without touching them.

Aristotle Best Quotes:

"Excellence is never an accident. It is always the result of high intention, sincere effort, and intelligent execution; it represents the wise choice of many alternatives - choice, not chance, determines your destiny."

"A friend to all is a friend to none."

"All human beings, by nature, desire to know."

"Anybody can become angry – that is easy, but to be angry with the right person and to the right degree and at the right time and for the right purpose, and in the right way – that is not within everybody's power and is not easy."

"Educating the mind without educating the heart is no education at all."

"Excellence is an art won by training and habituation. We do not act rightly because we have virtue or excellence, but we rather have those because we have acted rightly. We are what we repeatedly do. Excellence, then, is not an act but a habit."

"Happiness is an expression of the soul in considered actions."

"He who has never learned to obey cannot be a good commander."

"Quality is not an act it is a habit."

"It is during our darkest moments that we must focus to see the light."

"Through discipline comes freedom."

"It is not enough to win a war; it is more important to organize the peace."

"Knowing yourself is the beginning of all wisdom."

"To love someone is to identify with them."

The Epicurean and Stoic Philosophy in Psychology:

Epicureanism and Stoicism are philosophies that you can apply in your everyday life, compared to Platonism which is more about ideas. It's not a secret, that Stoics and Epicureans disagreed about many things and had a lot of debates. The Epicureans tried to avoid pain and found the necessary pleasure while the Stoics believed that are many things outside of our control in life and cared more about virtuous behavior. In my opinion, if you combine Epicureanism and Stoicism you make the perfect Philosophy and a cure for many diseases like anxiety, depression, etc.

The Epicurean Philosophy:

Epicurus was born in Samos in 431 BC. and was an Athenian citizen. Some of his teachers were the Platonic philosopher Pamfilos from Samos, the Xenocrates of the Academy in Athens, and the Aristotelian Praxifanis. At the age of thirty, after fulfilling his military obligations, he moved to Lesvos and founded a philosophical school. In 306 BC, Epicurus moved his school to Athens, renaming it "The Garden," and stayed there the rest of his life. The Garden was open to people of all ages, men, women, prostitutes, and slaves. Epicurus believed in positivity and that humans should be doing things that make them happy. For Epicurus hedonism was more about simplicity. For example, if someone is starving and finally eats, but in moderation, he will feel satisfied "ataraxia", but if he eats more, he will feel fatigued. Epicurus once said, when I say that the purpose of life is pleasure, I do not mean the pleasure of sensual pleasures. We should not suffer physical or emotional pain. Ataraxia for Epicurus is deeply connected with moral principles and ethics. If someone is unethical, he/she will suffer psychological trauma. The Epicurean Tetra-pharmakos "four-part remedy" is the path to eudaimonia: 'Don't fear god', 'don't worry about death', 'what is good is easy to get', 'what is terrible is easy to endure'. Also, we can't find eudemonia without the four-part virtues: 'Prudence', 'Bravery', 'Abstinence', and 'Justice'. According to Epicurus the pursuit of pleasure comes from human desires. Desires are not bad if we filter them through balance, moderation, and ethics. He separates desires into three categories, the desires that are natural and necessary such as food, health, friendship, and so on. The desires that are natural but not necessary like art, travel, etc. Finally, the desires that are neither natural nor necessary like greed, vanity, desires for glory and money, etc.

For Epicurus, a beggar may be more important than a rich or a celebrity person. Epicurus believed in utilitarianism. We need to be ethical and moral with others because is beneficial for us, as ethics is a path to eudaimonia. We feel pleasure from the happiness of our fellow human beings. Epicureanism had many crypto-Aristotelian ideas and influence the world and humanity in many ways.

The Epicurean Philosophy as Psychotherapy:

The psychologist Irvin D. Yalom a pioneer in the area of existential psychotherapy once said: In my work, "I consider my spiritual fathers not the great psychologists and psychiatrists of the 19th and 20th centuries, but the classical Greek philosophers and mainly Epicurus". For Irvin D. Yalom, Epicurus was the first cognitive psychotherapist. In Epicurean schools, a teacher observed the behavior and words of a student and criticized him/her honestly. This method helped the Epicureans to heal the soul through constructive criticism "psychotherapy". With the practice of epicurean psychotherapy, the teachers helped the students to correct their behavior mistakes. Irvin D. Yalom used to say: "If Epicurus were speaking to you at this moment, he would urge you to simplify life. Don't complicate your life with such trivial goals as riches and fame, those are the enemy of ATARAXIA". Modern psychology today goes in two directions one is the Epicurean and the other is the Neoplatonic. Recent psychoanalytic research has shown that death is the mother of all human fears. Epicurus said that Humans have two main fears, the fear of Gods and the fear of death. For achieving ataraxia (I'm my opinion, Epicurean ataraxia is similar to eudaimonia) we need to stop these fears. Epicurus believed in Gods, but Gods, according to him, are not involved with humans and have no influence over their lives. Death for Epicurus marks the end of consciousness and sensation. "Death is nothing to us, because as long as we exist, death is not here. And when it does come, we no longer exist." Friedrich Nietzsche once said: "Modern science confirms Epicurus every day". For Epicurus philosophy is useless if cannot treat the soul and mind, as medicine is useless if cannot cure the body. I'm going to close with a famous Epicurean quote: (λάθε βιώσας - lathe biōsas) - live secretly. Go through life without being noticed and maintain your inner peace. This point of view is diametrically opposed to today's society, where fame and recognition are almost required in everyday reality and virtual social media.

"Self-sufficiency is the greatest wealth of all" and "the greatest fruit of self-sufficiency is freedom".

"If you want to make Pythocles rich", Epikouros once advised, "do not give him more money, reduce his desires". Because bliss is an inner victory that transcends external circumstances.

The Stoic Philosophy:

Stoicism was born in Athens, at the beginning of the 3rd century BC. The Cypriot philosopher Zeno was the founder of Stoicism and the term "stoic" takes its name from the Stoa Poikile (Painted porch), a porch near the public market in Athens, which was Zeno's place of teachings. The difference with other philosophical schools of ancient Greece is that Stoicism still finds many admirers today. To put it simply, stoicism helps us to find the best in life.

"All things are parts of one single system, which is called nature, the individual life is good when it is in harmony with nature." – Zeno of Citium

Stoicism is an ancient self-help guide that has stood the test of time and is now more relevant than ever. The Stoic philosophy reduces negative emotions, increases positive ones, enhances cognitive performance, and overall satisfaction. This philosophy experienced glorious times during the Roman Empire, with prominent representatives such as the emperor Marcus Aurelius, Epictetus, and the orator and politician Seneca. According to Stoicism, man's duty is self-control, discipline, and to put himself in harmony with the Universe, which, as pure divine, transfers its properties to him. The ultimate goal is inner peace and liberation from suffering. Stoics had two main rules, judgment and observation (intention). We have to observe our thoughts and judge right from wrong, based on our instincts. The main instinct of humans is Virtue. Virtue is the only way to make the right decision.

Through Stoicism, we can distinguish the facts that we can control from those in which we have no power. If we cannot control what happens in our lives, we can control our reaction to these events and react either productively or destructively or even with apathy.

The Stoic Influence on Cognitive Psychotherapy:

As I mentioned many times philosophers are the physicians of the soul and CBT is deeply indebted to Stoic philosophers. Stoics referred to themselves as a Socratic sect. Socrates for the Stoics was an example of human inner strength and a great teacher. The influence of Socrates on Zeno was mediated by the Cynic philosophy. The Socratic-Cynic schools had a strong influence on Stoic philosophy. Diogenes the Cynic was like an "emperor" for stoics as he was a master of Self-Discipline and self-control. Stoicism and CBT have in common, logic, and critical thinking to overcome emotional difficulties.

Stoics attempted to incorporate Aristotelian logic and physics into their philosophy. For example, ten people listen to a man talking about something simple, like, "there is a river and it has a lot of fish". Among these ten, the majority will hear the speech from different perspectives and will give a different interpretation. So it's not what we hear but how we react to it. As Epictetus once said: "*It's not what happens to you, but how you react to it that matters*". Assume someone calls you fool in a language you don't understand, such as Ancient Sanskrit. You will react to this insult? No, as the sound is just an acoustic stimulus. So again, it is not what we hear but how we react that matters. Like Lucius Annaeus Seneca said: "*We suffer more in imagination than in reality.*" For me, this quote is an antidote to anxiety. Albert Ellis, an American psychologist who in 1955 developed Rational Emotive Behavior Therapy, admitted that many of the central principles of Rational Emotive Behavior Therapy were originally discovered by the Stoics. Epictetus was perhaps Albert Elli's biggest source of inspiration. In the 1960s, Aaron Temkin Beck another American psychiatrist who is professor emeritus in the department of psychiatry at the University of Pennsylvania mentioned the influence of Stoics on his ideas.

Stoic Meditation Practices:

The goal of Stoic meditation is not the same as that of Eastern meditation awareness, which is to achieve mental stillness. Stoic meditation is more of an exercise for clear thinking. A Stoic will not rush to judgment or react to everything he hears or sees. While Buddhism meditation teaches us to live in the Present Moment. Stoic meditation teaches us sometimes the opposite, to not be in the Present Moment if there is suffering and pain or to be positive when this happens. As Marcus Aurelius said: *Today I escaped anxiety. Or no, I discarded it, because it was within me, in my own perceptions— not outside.* Here are some Stoic meditation practices.

Disasters Practice:

If something bad happens to you start imagining the worst that could befall you, as if happening now, while keeping your Stoic impartiality. Start thinking about what is up to you and what is not, and what is the best you can do about it. Remind yourself that the only things you can control are your thoughts and your actions.

Morning Practice - Adopt your Virtues:

First of all, be positive and grateful that you woke up this morning, as many people will not have this privileged. Start scheduling how you will adopt your virtues and how to avoid your vices. As an example, I will pick a philosophical virtue like temperance. Now, try to cultivate temperance and include it in your day.

Finally, start to imagine what difficult situations may arise today and how to deal with them.

Death Study Practice
(Meleti Thanatou - Μελέτη θανάτου):

We are mortals, and we have no control over it. It's normal and inevitable. Some days remind yourself that this day could be your last. Try to live in the present moment, and respect the gift of life.

A View from Above Practice:

This practice is to give us a sense of the bigger picture and to remind us about how small we really are. Most of the things we worry about are not important when you start to imagine the whole world as seen from high above. Think about a problem you have and how small your problem is when looking at it from above the clouds.

Epictetus The Art of Living:

Epictetus is very important for Stoicism. Was Born in Phrygia around 55 AD and died in 135 AD. For many years was a slave and belonged to the Roman citizen Epaphroditus. Epaphroditus tested many times the stoic limits of Epictetus. It is said that once Epaphroditus twisted the foot of Epictetus and broke it! Epictetus smiled and answered him: "You see, I told you it would break"! After that, Epaphroditus set him free and Epictetus devoted entirely to philosophy.

Epictetus, like Socrates, never wrote anything. Fortunately, one of his students, Arrian of Nicomedia "Flavio Arriano", published eight books on Epictetus's philosophy "The Dissertations on Epictetus". Arrian selected the most essential ones and compiled them in a small book known as the Enchiridion "Handbook". Epictetus's philosophical ideas are considered the root of the modern term, "behavioral self-management" in psychology.

Great Quotes by Epictetus:

"There is only one way to happiness and that is to cease worrying about things which are beyond the power of our will".

"We have two ears and one mouth so that we can listen twice as much as we speak".

"The key is to keep company only with people who uplift you, whose presence calls forth your best."

"It's not what happens to you, but how you react to it that matters".

"Man is disturbed not by things, but by the views he takes of them".

"Man is not worried by real problems so much as by his imagined anxieties about real problems"

"No man is free who is not master of himself".

"Only the educated are free"

"Never depend on the admiration of others. There is no strength in it. Personal merit cannot be derived from an external source. It is not to be found in your personal associations, nor can it be found in the regard of other people. It is a fact of life that other people, even people who love you, will not necessarily agree with your ideas, understand you, or share your enthusiasms. Grow up! Who cares what other people think about you!"

"People who do not philosophize blame others, a man who has begun to philosophize blame himself, but a real philosopher blames neither others nor himself". - Epictetus (Book: The Art of Living).

Apollonius of Tyana - The Great Healer:

Apollonius of Tyana is recognized as a divine Man. People called him Theos Aner. Theos Aner literally means (θείος ανήρ) divine men. The Arabic writers called him Aka Balinas which means demigod. The Roman emperor-philosopher Marcus Aurelius admired Apollonius, saying "From Apollonius I have learned freedom of will and understanding, the steadiness of purpose, and to look to nothing else, not even for a moment, except to reason." Voltaire spoke about Apollonius in the highest terms. Eunapius, the pupil of Chrysanius said "Apollonius was more than a philosopher, he was a middle term, as it were, between gods and men. From a young age, he gave great speeches and people were gathering at the temples to listen to him. Apollonius was a healthy man with a strong physique and lived to the ripe age of 98 years old. He was strictly vegetarian, He healed the sick and performed many miracles like exorcisms of demons and raising the dead. Hierocles at the start of the fourth century boldly charged the Christian priesthood their plagiarism of the teachings of Apollonius. The ancient Greeks pioneered the practice of physiognomy. Pythagoras used physiognomy knowledge in students based on how gifted they looked. Apollonius during his Pythagorean period of silence traveled and communicated silently with many people. He learned to communicate with gestures and with body language. Finally, He shared this physiognomic wisdom with some Indian philosophers, who were also similar to Pythagoras, and select their students by observation of their physical characteristics

(VA 2.30). Unfortunately, every vestige of written information about Apollonius was destroyed, when the great libraries of Alexandra and Cordoba burnt down. Eight books were written between 170 and 245 AD by the Greek sophist Lucius Flavius Philostratus, who chronicles the life of Apollonius of Tyana. Flavius Philostratus was summoned by the Roman empress Julia Domna, who had with her the diary of his disciple Damis of Nineveh. She got the diary from a close relative of Damis.

Summary of Philostratus 8 Books:

Book 1: Philostratus describes Apollonius's birth and youth and how he become a Pythagorean and devotee of Askclepio. In search of wisdom, he travels to Assyria and met Damis of Nineveh his most faithful follower. They travel to India and visit the Brahmanas.

Book 2: Apollonius continued his journey to India and at the city of Taxila he meets the wise Indian King Phraotes.

Book 3: In the third book, Apollonius meets the Indian Wise Men and their leader Iarchas.

Book 4: Apollonius returns to Greece. He visited many cities on the mainland. In these places, He gives lectures and performs miracles. Later, he travels to Rome in Nero's time and to Spain.

Book 5: After spending some time in Spain, Apollonius and his friends made their way to Alexandria. At Alexandria he encounters Vespasian, the future Rome emperor.

Book 6: Apollonius travels south to visit "the naked ones" that are located south of Thebes. After the adventure with the Gymnosophists, he returns to Alexandria and continues around the Mediterranean.

Book 7: In Rome, Apollonius was arrested and brought to trial as a result of his lectures against tyranny and against

Domitian. He is trying to defend himself against the charges but Domitian threw him back into prison.

Book 8: In the next trial Apollonius is acquitted, and magically disappears from the courthouse. He meets Damis and Dimitrios outside of Rome. He then returns to Greece, where Philostratus describes his death and its appearance in a young man's dream to prove the soul's immortality.

Appolonius Travels:

According to Philostratus Apollonius traveled to many countries. Some of them were Italy, Hispania, Egypt, Ethiopia Nubia, Mesopotamia, India, and Nepal. But why Apollonius traveled around the world? If you read about the life of Pythagoras you will find many similarities with the life of Apollonius. Apollonius was a big fan of Pythagoras and was influenced by him. Pythagoras was initiated by many mystics from around the world, saw many rituals, and learned all the healing secrets of the alchemists. For the same reason Apollonius was also traveled around the known world. Here are some important adventures of Apollonius.

The Journey to India:

In Vita Apollonii of Philostratus, Damis describes the visit to India. It is a genuine account of India and the only one that came to us from the old world in a complete state. The story of Apollonius in India reminds us the Marco Polo's travels, but with more spirituality. Apollonius visited the wise men of India who were called "Indian Brahmans". Iarchas was the leader of the Indian Wise Men. When Apollonius explored the Wise Men's city, he discovers that the city contains sacred statues from India, Greece, and Egypt. That's not surprising after all, as after the invasion of Alexander the Great we have the Indo-Greek art and the Greco-Buddhism that I mentioned also in the Pankration chapter. Greco-Buddhism is the cultural syncretism between Hellenistic culture and Buddhism. In India, Demis describes many spiritual rituals and magic ceremonies like the deep well with the sacred water, and the crater of fire that gives a black flame, which Indians used to purify their accidental crimes. Iarchas also revealed the two magic jars to them. The first contained rainstorms and the second winds. In a letter that Apollonius wrote to the Egyptians, he described, "I saw the Indian Brahmans living on the earth and not on it, walled without walls, and with no possessions except the whole world". According to Philostratus, the Indian Brahmans slept on the ground, but the earth gave them beds of grass. In their religious rites to the Sun, the Wise Men could rise and hover in the air. Finally, even if they lived out in the open air, they could call shade for cover, protect themselves from rain, and summon sunshine whenever they want. During his visit to India, Apollonius healed many people and performed many mystical acts. The Brahmans had long hair held by a white band and walked barefoot. They wore a white cotton, one-sleeve tunic. Also, they had a lot of rings and carried a rod with magic powers. The rituals for the Sun were performed three times, at dawn, noon, and at midnight. Sometimes they rubbed an amber-colored ointment on their heads, which made their bodies warm to the point of steaming. At the temple, they sang a song, and when they hit the ground with their staffs they start levitating one meter from the ground. The greatest knowledge the Wise Men possessed was the ability to see an individual's past lives. Iarchas claim that anticipation makes men "divine" but requires a pure soul free of sin. The universe according to the Brahmanas composed of five elements: Water, air, earth, fire, and ether. Ether is the origin and breath of the gods. The universe is a living being and is both male and female.

The Journey to Egypt:

Apollonius after advising Vespasian in Alexandria traveled south to visit "the naked ones" that were located between Egypt's border and Ethiopia, south of Thebes. The "Gymnosophists" of Egypt, whom Damis called "naked Egyptian philosophers," is the name given by the Greeks to certain ancient Indian philosophers who pursued asceticism. The word "naked" probably meant "lightly clad." The gymnosophists in Egypt were called Ethiopean Gymnosophists by Apollonius of Tyana. Perhaps they were Buddhist missionaries who traveled westward. Apollonius, at last, spoke to philosophers who lived just like him. These Egyptian ascetics ate no foods of animal origin, practiced fasting, and were strict vegetarians. Some of the descriptions of gymnosophists match with Jain (Jainism) saints who do not eat the root of the vegetables to prevent injuring small insects and to prevent also the killing of the plant soul. They also exclude various types of green vegetables during some periods of the month. All living things contain a soul so they try to cause as little harm as possible to the plants. Some say that the sect of Therapeutae of Alexandria derived from them and mixed with Pythagoreans. Apollonius also claimed that the Naked Ones once supported Pythagoras. Philostratus writes that the Naked Ones lived on a hill not far from the bank of the Nile. The Naked Ones had no homes and lived under the open sky. For visitors, there was a small colonnade that functioned as a pension house. In the beginning, Apollonius was not so welcome in the village of the Naked Ones, as the Euphrates (An enemy of Apollonius) had told them that Apollonius had been slandering them. Apollonius admonished the Naked Ones not to believe what the Euphrates says and that they are fools to trust him. Apollonius declared that the climate in this region allows anyone to be naked. Also, introduces the Naked Ones as inferior in wisdom to the Indians, but wiser than the Egyptians. Apollonius assumed that the Indian Wise Men's superiority is a result of living in purer sun rays. The leader of the Naked Ones, Thespesion, replied to Apollonius that the Indian Wise Men only perform magic to demonstrate their power, such as levitation to tempt visitors. The Naked Ones don't need any of that. The earth in the land of gymnosophists is not forced to do anything against its will. They respect the earth and live off its natural products. Thespesion emphasized, that the Naked Ones have also the power to beguile, but the Naked Ones choose not to use these powers. The number one rule of the Cynic philosophy of the Naked Ones was that frugality is the teacher of wisdom and the teacher of truth.

Apollonius Books:

According to Suda encyclopedia and other sources he wrote the following works:

The Mystic Rites or Concerning Sacrifices:

Philostratus mentioned this book, as he came across copies of the book in many temples, cities, and libraries. Several fragments of it have been preserved, The most important to be found in Eusebius. Many scholars tell us that this book is genuine as it was widely circulated with high respect, and its rules were engraved on brazen pillars at Byzantium. When reading the Concerning Sacrifices it's obvious that Apollonius was the first who didn't like idolatry and sacrifices. Here is a small part of this book:

'Tis best to make no sacrifice to God at all, no lighting of a fire, no calling Him by any name that men employ for things to sense. For God is over all, the first; and only after Him do come the other Gods. For He doth stand in need of naught e'en from the Gods, much less from us small men — naught that the earth brings forth, nor any life she nurseth, or even anything the stainless air contains. The only fitting sacrifice to God is man's best reason, and not the word [logos]4 that comes from out his mouth. We men should ask the best of beings through the best thing in us, for what is good. I mean by means of mind, for mind needs no material things to make its prayer.So then, to God, the mighty One, who's over all, no sacrifice should ever be lit up.

The Secret of Creation:

This work comes from the Arabian world, (Jábir ibn Hayyán 722-815 - Kitáb al-'Ilal from the Book of Causes of Hermes). According to this book, while Apollonius explored a crypt beneath a statue of Hermes, he discovered both the Emerald Tablet of Hermes and the "Book of Causes". Philostratus's book (viii, 19-20), has a connecting story where Apollonius entered a cave at the temple of Trophonius in Greece and after seven days he returned to his friends carrying a book of philosophy similar to the teachings of Pythagoras.

According to Philostratus this book was later entrusted to the care of the emperor Hadrian and kept in his palace at Antium together with some letters of Apollonius.

The Oracles or Concerning Divination:

None possesses a copy of this rare work. This book is mentioned by Moeragenes and Damis and was based on what Apollonius had learned in India. Apollonius's divination was not ordinary astrology, but something that Philostratus considers higher than ordinary human art in such matters.

The Life of Pythagoras:

Apollonius was a big fan of Pythagoras, in his book about Pythagoras, Apollonius affirms that Pythagoras was the son of Apollo and Pythais. Porphyry refers to his work, and Iamblichus extracts a long passage from it.

The Will of Apollonius:

Philostratus mentioned this book. This book was written in the Ionic dialect and was a summary of Apollonius's doctrines.

The Great Book of Talismans:

The Great Book of Talismans (Kitāb al-ṭalāsim al-Akbar) is one of the Greek texts that have reached us in its Arabic recension. The talismans created by Apollonius were discovered in several cities of the Eastern Roman Empire but also in many other cities like Alexandria, Antioch, Emesa, Ephesus, and Edessa. They were magical figures, statues, or columns inscribed with magical names and erected in public places, either buried or placed on a high spots, and even sometimes protected by holy places. Were made to protect the cities from afflictions. These talismans were so famous that it was a challenge to the Christians. Some church fathers condemned them as demon sorcery well others admitted that such magic was beneficial, but none of them claimed that the talismans didn't work. Justin Martyr an early Christian apologist, philosopher, and great Father of the church of the 2nd century, said: 'How is it that the amulets of Apollonius have power over certain parts of creation because they can prevent, the fury of the waves, the intensity of the winds and the attacks of wild animals? And while the miracles of our Lord are preserved only by the Tradition, those of Apollonius, they are more numerous and are truly proven in present facts, so as to seduce everyone who sees them'.

Here is an important a passage from the book:

This is a noble science and If you want to successfully operate the wonders that you are going to find in this book, then you have to abstain from every evil action, and above all from the conversation and the company of women. Fast, prayer, compassion, chastity, sincerity, and good opinion, in the name of God, the Mighty, the Sublime." - Apollonius of Tyana.

Apollonius of Tyana Epigram:

In the New Museum of Adana was found an epigram about Apollonius of Tyana that has significant historical importance. This is one of the most crucial pieces of evidence that Apollonius of Tyana had the fame of a divine Man.

Αυτός ο άνθρωπος ονομάστηκε ετσι προς τιμήν του Απόλλωνα, Και έλαμψε στα Τιάνα σβήνοντας τα λάθη (ελαττώματα) των ανθρώπων. Ο τάφος του στα Τυάνα έλαβε το σώμα του αλλά στην πραγματικότητα ο ουρανός τον έλαβε ούτως ώστε να μπορέσει να διώξει έξω τον πόνο των ανθρώπων.

Epigram Translation:
'This man, named in honor of Apollo, and shining forth Tyana, extinguished the faults of men. The tomb in Tyana (received) his body, but in truth heaven received him so that he might drive out the pains of men.

Apollonius of Tyana Quotes and Prayer:

The Daily Prayer of Apollonius:

In Ancient Greek:

Ηλιε, πεμπε με εφ' οσον της γης εμοι τε και σοι δοκει, και
γιγνωσκοιμι ανδρας αγαθους, φαυλους δε μητε εγω
μαθοιμι μητε εμε φαυλοι.»

In English:

*Sun, lead me to whatever part of the earth we both like.
Make me recognize the good people, and the bad neither
to know them nor know me".*

Apollonius of Tyana Quotes:

*"The bad people do not sacrifice or give offers to
honor the gods but to buy out the punishment"*.

*"The gods certainly know the future, the people the
events and the wise the approaching."*

*"The soul that does not take care to learn self-
sufficiency in the body, can not become self-sufficient
either."*

*"Most of the people of their own mistakes become
advocates, but in mistakes of others are becoming
prosecutors."*

"As for me, I am not interested in any kind of regime, because I live under the roof of the gods, but I do not consider it right for the human herd to wear out in the absence of justice and a prudent buccaneer."

"The most important people are very brief in their speech. The loquacious, if they were tired as they drain the others, they would not speak at length".

"In the cycle of the Sun, many things become visible every time that rises".

"It is at the time of dawn that we must commune with the gods."

"All the earth is mine, and I have a right to go all over it and through it.
"

"In my judgment, excellence and wealth are direct opposites, since when the one shrinks, the other grows, and when one grows, the other shrinks."

"Pythagoras said that the most divine art was that of healing. And if the healing art is most divine, it must occupy itself with the soul as well as with the body; for no creature can be sound so long as the higher part in it is sickly."

"Apollonius of Tyana said about Aesop: "Like those who dine well off the plainest dishes, he made use of humble incidents to teach great truths".

"Death does not exist for anyone, except apparently, nor does birth exist for anyone, except apparently. The change of essence into nature is considered birth, while the change of nature into essence is considered death. Nothing is truly born or ever worn out, only one becomes visible and then invisible. Everything changes into parts, and parts into the whole due to the unity of everything". **Apollonius of Tyana - Letter To Valerius [About life and death].**

.

Theology of the Ancient Greek Philosophers:

Theology in ancient Greece was polytheistic, there were numerous gods and goddesses, but if you study Greek philosophy you will realize that the ancient Greeks believed in "one" God. The Pythagorean Unit is the term given by the Pythagoreans for God or the primary "Being". The number One is symbolizing unity. Pythagoreanism is derived from Orphism and has many similarities with Hinduism. Metempsychosis of souls was one of their fundamental beliefs. The gods of ancient Greeks were involved in every element of human existence. The gods were arranged in a hierarchy, with Zeus, the king of the gods, ruling over all the rest. The ancient Greek gods represent archetypal forces of nature and manifest in our world in a variety of ways. They bring order and harmony to our material world. These symmetrical forces of the cosmos emanate from Zeus' cosmic mind. What I do want you to realize is that the Greek priests did not invent the gods.

Their minds evolved to these transcendental stages and through initiation, a significant part of the truth was revealed to them. Greek theo-philosophers uncovered the Greek religion and created the language, for that reason, the Greek language is conceptual. Through the mysteries, Greek mythology was also created. The Greek priests essentially obtained their knowledge from the good demons of the golden race, who were the only entities below the gods and are able to get access to all secrets. Thus, the Greek theo-philosophers and legislators gave the forces of creation, or gods, names that represented and explained their essence. Greek mythology is a codified science that explains the nature of the universe. Some examples of personifications of the forces of nature are the wind deities. Aeolus, Boreas, Notus, Eurus, and Zephyrus. The goddess Athena personifies wisdom and righteousness. Hermes, known as Mercury by the Romans is the Greek god of trade, communication, and travel. Aphrodite is the Greek goddess of sexual pleasure, love and beauty and was known by the Romans as Venus and so on... Our today astrology is surrounded by the greatness of the ancient gods. The words Dias (Dias is the Greek word for Zeus - Dio in Latin means god. Dio in Greek means two) and Zeus "ζευξη" (which in Greek means combine) symbolize the universal force that divides and unites everything.

As previously stated, the Greek language is conceptual; for example, many of the words in Greek and even in English (since English is derived from Greek) include the word Dia "Zeus" (Dias essentially symbolizes the cosmic mind). Here are a few examples:

"Dia-spora = Zeus seeds"
"Dia-gnosis = Zeus knowledge"
"Dia-fragma= Zeus barrier"
"Dia-logos = Zeus's speech"
"Dia-vállo = I fight against Zeus" and he who fights against Zeus is... diabolos - "devil".
"Meditation - Dia-logismos= Zeu's thinking"

The Demigods:

Numerous Demigods existed in ancient Greece. For example, Zeus had many children with mortal women. The most know Demigods are Heracles: Son of Zeus and Alcmene, Achilles: Son of the sea nymph Thetis, Asclepius: Son of Apollo and Coronis, Dionysus: Son of Zeus and Semele, Theseus: Son of Poseidon and Aethra, and even Great Alexander: Who was considered to be the son of the god Zeus Ammon in Egypt. Olympias, Alexander's mother, trained as a priestess in Samothrace. Alexander was taught a lot about the metaphysical from his mother and realized from an early age that although Philip might be his biological father, he also possessed supernatural abilities. The Temple of Samothrace is said to be where Philip first fell in love with Olympias. After marrying Olympias, King Philip had a dream in which he placed a seal with the emblem of a lion on her belly. Aristandros of Telmessos predicted that his wife was pregnant and carrying a child with the strength of a lion.

In Egypt, the Persian occupying forces surrendered unconditionally, and the Egyptian people welcomed Alexander as a savior from the Persian tyranny. The Egyptians immediately crowned him Pharaoh. Alexander made that "epic" march from Memphis to the Ammon Shiva oasis out of a deep religious need. The prophet in the sanctuary addressed Alexander the Great as the son of Ammon Zeus, which Alexander believed was a revelation of the god himself. Additionally, according to legend, Alexander the Great possessed the Shield of Achilles made by Hephaestus and the Thunderbolt of Zeus. In conclusion, Demigods had divine qualities and were endowed with gifts from birth. For instance, being the son of Aphrodite implied that the individual was exceedingly sensuous, attractive, and endowed with seducing abilities. Before these gifted children were born, the gods frequently appeared in visions or dreams of the parents.

To be completely honest, I was unsure whether or not to write the content that follows. My mother had a dream the night before I was born in which the goddess Athena told her that a significant Greek would be born. This was quite odd because my mother had no relation to ancient Greece, but on the contrary, she had Christian beliefs. When she describes the dream to us, my sisters often chuckle and calling me a philosopher (because I often talk about Greek philosophy). As I was taking my daily walk, I was debating whether or not to include this incident in the book. I knew it sounded very imagined, as well as blasphemous, to believe that I had received gifts from the goddess. Then it occurred to me to ask the goddess Athena herself if she wanted me to mention it or not.

I made an "internal monologue" and I said, goddess Athena if you want me to mention the incident with the dream, show me a sign. Show me a sign that I can recognize as being from you, such as the wise owl, which represents you. I was looking for signs as I walked. A part of me was convinced that what I had been thinking was completely ridiculous. The other part of me, on the other hand, knew that the gods existed (I had another incident in Delphi, which I will mention later) and that are cosmic forces of the universe. As I was thinking, I suddenly found myself on a street I used to walk down every day, and there, in a Coaching Center named αξία - "value," I came across the wise owl. I couldn't believe my eyes. First of all, how is it possible for me to pass by it every day and not see the owl? Second, if it was a coincidence, how did I manage to pass by at the appropriate time? My eyes welled up. I was touched by happiness, but at the same time I didn't know if it was just a coincidence, or a genuine encounter with the divine. _My Explanation_: From my perspective, it's obvious that they didn't place the owl in Coaching Center just for me. What actually happened, was a result of an inspiration that I experienced while I was thinking about this god's chapter. The divine brought to mind the story of my mother's dream while also verifying its existence. Additionally, I realized how interconnected everything is.

Some of you may be thinking at this time, "But everything he describes is pagan and belongs in the past." Try to expand your horizons, Christianity and Islam both, claim that there is only one God, but is this really true? As I state before, the Divine is something we don't understand fully. Although it cannot be defined, it can be known. It is everything and nothing, complete but empty, one and many. I sought spirituality and a connection to the divine throughout all of my research and journeys. I've witnessed a lot of unusual things, particularly in Asia and South America, and I'm aware that all major religions and spiritual traditions contain elements of the divine. However, the truth is that no matter how hard I looked elsewhere, the Greek cosmogony was where I found the transcendent the most. Even while I am aware that when people talk about divine beings in our times, they sound like they are speaking a language from another planet, I am also aware that the divine is kept hidden from the naive. Since they share similar principles, let's use Islam, Christianity, and Judaism as examples. In the Old Testament the word 'Elohim is the plural form of the word 'elohah (god). So, in Genesis, God is addressed in the plural. When God created man, He did not say, "Let me make man ", but said, "Let us make man." For the Father said, 'Let us make man in Our image and likeness.'The word "Elohim," which means "gods," is also written in the Torah, the Holy Bible's original source. In the whole Bible summarily, God is referred to as gods (Elohim) over 2,500 times. The gods share many similarities in mythologies around the world. The reason for this was that people in the past were more in touch with nature and had more contact with the transcendent. When we eliminated the gods from our lives and destroyed their temples, this to a certain extent, symbolizes man's aversion to nature.

Athena the Goddess Of Wisdom and Philosophy:

You don't believe that the gods represent the archetype forces of nature? Here is an example. The origins of Athens are lost in time, with records dating back to 3,200 BC. Aktiki was the first name of the city, given by its first king, Aktaeus. The second name was Kerkopia from King Cecrops. Cecrops accepted the goddess Athena's gift of the sacred olive tree, in 410 BC. According to folklore, two gods fought over who would rule the city when it was first established. Tradition tells us that Poseidon and Athena fought because they both wanted to claim the city as their own. Zeus recommended that each of them provide a gift to the city and whoever made the greatest would take the city under his protection. They selected Cecrops to judge this contest. The proposition was approved by the gods. First, Poseidon hit the Acropolis rock with his trident at one point, causing it to erupt with salty water that was later named "The Sea of Erechtheus," Athena responded by planting an olive tree on the Acropolis. Cecrops accepted this gift and from that time, the goddess Athena was the protector of the city. Why do we fail to see what's in plain sight? Prior to 410 BC, Athens was merely an ordinary city. The city of Athens instantly became the center of philosophy and knowledge from the moment goddess Athena took the city under her protection.

The Immortal Gods:

On the one hand, Gods represent the elements of nature and on the other hand, they were Humanoid but not mortal. After all, gods can take any form they want. But what exactly makes the gods immortal? As revealed in ancient myths, immortality can be achieved by eating certain foods. Ambrosia was a liquid food like oil and in addition to food, the gods used it to purify the body. Nectar, the drink of the gods, was twelve times sweeter than honey and it looked like red wine. Mortals required special divine favor in order to eat ambrosia and nectar. In my opinion, the comparison of the gods to the mortal realm, suggests that man with the proper knowledge he can become a demigod, a deity, or one with the gods.

Hades and the Kingdom of the Dead:

Hades in Greek means the world that has no matter. as mentioned above, the ancient Greeks believed in Metempsychosis (reincarnation). Every time someone dies their soul goes to Hades. The judgment takes place in Hades and the soul undergoes testing before reincarnating in order to grow lighter and progress to higher levels. In a way, Hades functions as a reformatory of souls. We all experience rebirth because the soul needs matter to bring out actions. Depending on how light or dark the soul is, it is transferred to one of the three realms of hades. The Elysian Fields are the upper level, where the most virtuous and lighter souls go. The valley, is the middle level, where the majority of souls go, and Tartarus is the third and worst level. The souls are punished in Tartarus according to the crimes they committed. In order to avoid acting in the same way when reincarnating. In each incarnation, the soul, according to mythology and philosophy, temporarily loses its memory. The souls nevertheless, will carry all of their good and bad qualities with them and have to act righteously in the material world. Memory loss is necessary because, if the soul were to remember its former incarnations, it would act morally out of fear rather than free will. Mnemosyne was one of the most important Pythagorean goddesses, according to Apollonius of Tyana. Through awakening, highly evolved souls can regain their memory. Many philosophers, including Pythagoras, were able to remember their prior lives. A soul reaches perfection only when it is identified with the divine.

Delphi - Temple of Apollo:

To understand more about the ancient Greek religion, I had to visit a place that was believed to be the center (navel) of the Earth and to explore more about the god of light, Apollo. Delphi was a sacred site devoted to the Greek deity Apollo. When we arrived by bus a terrible storm started and there were black clouds everywhere. I didn't have the right clothes and I only had three hours until the next bus to Athens. As funny as it may seem, I prayed to Apollo:

Hail Apollo god of light if I'm welcome here please bring the light and stop the storm.

I don't know if it was just a coincidence but two minutes after my prayer the sun was shining brightly and the clouds completely went away. My travel companion was shocked when what I had predicted actually happened and claimed it was unnatural, because there were dark clouds everywhere.

The word "Delphi" comes from the Greek word "Delphus," which means "hollow" or "womb." According to the legend, two eagles were released into the skies by the Greek god Zeus. One bird went east while the other went west, after flying around the world, the two birds finally reunited in Delphi. Omphalos is the Delphic name for the location where they met. The navel-stone was the symbol of Delphi and is an ancient marble monument that was found at the archaeological site of Delphi. Pythia was the name of the high priestess of the Temple. In the beginning was a pure, innocent, and honest young virgin that was chosen to serve as a bridge between this world and the next. Later, older ladies, at least 50 years old, began to occupy the position, clothed in traditional virginal garb. Plutarch, the historian middle Platonist philosopher, biographer, and priest at the Temple of Apollo in Delphi attributed Pythia's prophetic powers to vapors that may have arisen from a cleft in the earth.

The Charioteer of Delphi is called Iniohos in the Greek language and means "he who holds the reins".

This statue is said to have been made in the 5th century BC by Pythagoras. It probably represents Plato's Chariot Allegory. Plato was influenced by Pythagoras' teachings and compared the higher part of the soul to a person driving a chariot pulled by two wild horses. Those two horses are the lower parts of the soul and depict desires.

The Diet of the Greek Philosophers:

We know without a doubt that Orphics and Pythagoreans such as Apollonius of Tyana, Iamblichus, etc. were strict vegetarians, but the majority of all philosophers, including Socrates, Diogenes, Heraclitus, Aristotle, Thales, Hippocrates, and others, were vegetarians as well. Diogenes the Cynic recommended vegetarianism as a way to reduce sexual desire, an opinion also shared by Platonic Socrates. Glaucon was Plato's older brother who, like him, was a member of Socrates' inner circle of students. In Plato's Republic, Socrates debates with Glaucon about the city's diet and the implications of vegetarianism versus carnivorism.

Socrates: I suggest that the cities be retained simple, Glaucon. Citizens should eat wheat, barley with salt, olives, and cheese, as well as the traditional dish of boiled onions and cabbage. For dessert, I suggests figs, peas, beans, roasted blueberries, hazelnuts, and wine.

Glaucon: *Socrates, citizens should live in a "civilized manner," not on a "pig diet". To enjoy modern dishes and desserts while relaxing on sofas. In other words, to be able to buy meat.*

Socrates: *If you desire a city that will suffer from inflammations, we will need large quantities of all kinds of animals, to be eaten by the citizens who desire them... Isn't that right?*

Glaucon: *Of course we will need.*

Socrates: *As a result, more doctors will be needed than with the diet I suggested before.*

Glaucon: *Indeed, that's accurate.*

Socrates: *Because large pasture areas will be required to raise so many animals, this luxurious state will be limited in size. Due to a lack of land, violent situations may arise, necessitating the intervention of justice to deal with the violence. "When disease and licentiousness abound in a city, there will be more physicians and lawyers!"*

Pythagorean Diet:

The Pythagorean diet included fruits, vegetables, cereals, a little dairy, and a little wine. What we call the Pythagorean diet is actually a Lacto-vegetarian diet, conducive to the preservation of health, and the cure of diseases. The famous Pythagorean cup was designed with a column in the middle of the cup. This cup is spilling the drink when a person is too greedy. The purpose of the cup was the indication of the golden mean, " MODERATION IS BEST".

The famous Pythagorean Apollonius of Tyana thought that meat-eating was dirty and bad for the mind. He ate nuts, fruits vegetables, and wild greens, saying that these foods are pure and come from mother earth. He mostly ate fresh vegetables and Tragimata (τραγήματα). Tragimata in ancient Greece were mainly fresh or dried fruits, nuts such as walnuts, and sweets made with honey. Dried figs were a very popular Tragimata for our ancestors. About wine, He said that is a pure drink, as it comes from a plant, but that contradicts the components of the mind because it obscures the ethereal nature of the soul. One day a King wanted to satisfy Apollonius and for that reason, he called him for dinner. When Apollonius arrived the King's table was full of vegetables, seeds, fruits, and nuts, but when Apollonius saw it he told him that he preferred wild from the forest and not cultivated.

"As long as Man continues to be the ruthless destroyer of lower living beings, he will never know health or peace. For as long as men massacre animals, they will kill each other. Indeed, he who sows the seed of murder and pain cannot reap joy and love." -Pythagoras.

Plutarch Wellness and Flesh-Eating:

Plutarch as mentioned was a Greek Middle Platonist philosopher and biographer that spent the last thirty years of his life serving as a high priest in Delphi. Plutarch is one of the most influential writers who ever lived, he produced over 200 works. He traveled extensively in Greece and Asia Minor and visited Alexandria, Egypt. Plutarch was very much concerned with morality in an age when men were losing their faith in religion and philosophy. He wrote on health matters such as vegetarianism and diet, as well as spiritual topics like divine justice, sacred prophecies, demonology, and mysticism.

Philosophy as Soul Medicine:
"Philosophy, should be the head of education. For the care of the body, people invented two sciences, medicine and gymnastics. The first gives people health and the

second implanting wellness to humans. But for the diseases and passions of the soul the only cure is philosophy. Through Philosophy we can know what is good and what is bad, what is right and what is wrong, and in general what choices to make in life and what to avoid. I think these are the greatest goods that philosophy has to offer." – Models od Education – Plutarch

Vegetarianism:

"*You ask of me then for what reason it was that Pythagoras abstained from eating of flesh. I for my part do much admire in what humor, with what soul or reason, the first man with his mouth touched slaughter, and reached to his lips the flesh of a dead animal, and having set before people courses of ghastly corpses and ghosts, could give those parts the names of meat and victuals, that but a little before lowed, cried, moved, and saw.*""*But you who live now, what madness, what frenzy drives you to the pollution of shedding blood, you who have such a superfluity of necessities? Why slander the earth by implying that she cannot support you? Why impiously offend law-giving Demeter and bring shame upon Dionysus, lord of the cultivated vine,the gracious one, as if you did not receive enough from their hands? Are you not ashamed to mingle domestic crops with blood and gore? You call serpents and panthers and lions savage, but you yourselves, by your own foul slaughters, leave them no room to outdo you in cruelty; for their slaughter is their living, yours is a mere appetizer.* – " On the eating of flesh – Plutarch.

According to Plutarch, Human anatomy is not designed for both the consumption and the assimilation of meat. It is out of human nature to eat blood foods since we cannot support such a diet. Unlike carnivores, man cannot kill an animal with his own hands without the help of weapons or tools he has made. Humans cannot easily digest blood and are forced to cook their meat instead of eating it raw, like animals.

"The construction of the body demonstrates that eating meat is not in man's nature. There are no protruding lips, pointed nails, sharp teeth, a strong stomach, and warm breath capable of transmuting and processing heavy meat ingredients. If you claim to be made for this type of food, first kill what you want to eat by yourself, without the use of any tool but only your hands " - Plutarch.

"What we eat is extremely important, but so is how much we consume." – Evexiandros.

"The food we eat serves its purpose when we're digesting it, not when we're tasting it" - Musonius Rufus.

"The beginning and foundation of temperance lie in the self-control of eating and drinking." - Musonius Rufus.

"Whatever one eats becomes a part of him and has significant consequences." - Musonius Rufus.

Neoplatonism as a Therapy and Redemption of the Soul:

As I mentioned before Apollonius was a Neopythagorean Philosopher. Another great neo-Pythagorean philosopher was The Greek Numenius of Apamea that was also the forerunner of "Neoplatonism" and whose thought strongly influenced Plotinus, Porphyry, and many Christian thinkers. He was Platonic and Pythagorean at the same. The term Neoplatonism is not ancient, it is a "modern name" and a creation of Thomas Taylor (1758-1835). This philosophy belongs to the tradition of Platonic philosophy. Plotinus is practically the founder of "Neoplatonism," but, his teacher Ammonius Sakkas, who lived in Alexandria, Egypt was the first "Neoplatonist" philosopher. Plotinus ruled philosophically in his time and created the "Neoplatonic School," which influenced Christianity and Byzantium. Like Socrates, Ammonius never wrote anything, his life surrounded by mystery. After the death of Plotinus, his book Enneads published by his student Porphyry (232 - 301), became the foundation of the whole philosophical system of the "Neoplatonic" philosophers. Many ideas of Neo-Platonism were adopted by Christian thinkers, mainly Saint Augustine (354 - 430). Plotinus thought of himself as a simple interpreter of Plato. Plotinus believed that all reality derived from an essential principle called Agathon (good) or the One (En.) The ancient Greek philosophical term one means unity. One was at the top of the ontological pyramid and before the world of ideas. The one is indefinite. We cannot define it. It is not even possible to name it. Agathon (good) or the One (En) are just names that we give to describe it but without success. Plotinus argues that with Platonism, we found the ultimate goal of human life, to be one with the Devine (Perfection). This goal is achieved only when a man is moral and has virtues, such as wisdom, justice, piety, etc. Another (secret) way to achieve this, is the Platonic "***Philosophical Death***."

This is achieved when the soul through philosophy manages to liberate itself and achieve unification with the divine. Plato said after all: "Philosophy is the study of death." An example of philosophical death can be found in Plato's cave allegory. If one of the chained people of the cave manages to free himself from the cave and sees the sunlight, he will quickly understand the delusion in which he lived. Socrates explains that the philosopher is like a prisoner who has been freed from the shackles of delusion. In other words, philosophy functions as a cure and redemption of the soul.

Christianity and Hellenism:

"The purpose of this chapter is not to disturb your faith and beliefs but to help you seek the truth and to investigate the similarities and influence of Greek philosophy on Christianity. Honestly, I didn't want to write this chapter as it is very sensitive and to keep my book with purely philosophical facts on wellness issues, but I found so much information that I Couldn't resist sharing this knowledge with you. We live in dark times after all. I am not a pagan neither a Christian, but I am a man who seeks the divine and bliss with an open mind. I have dedicated my life to this quest, and I have traveled to many places in search of philosophy, especially in Asia, Europe, and South America. In any case, my research has led me there, and as a seeker of balance, I have a duty to present them."

After the persecution and ban of Philosophy, a new era was born in Rome. The era of Christianity. Therefore, Stoic, Pythagorean, and Cynic philosophical ideas are hidden within Christianity. In a way, Christianity is the destroyer and "continuation" of the Hellenistic spirituality. You will find the Greek philosophers, everywhere in Christianity especially in Orthodox Christianity.

Socrates and Plato as "Christ Prophets":

Most church fathers agree that the ancient Greek philosophers "prophesied" the coming of the Messiah. The question now is why there is nothing in Judaism that foretells the crucifixion of the messiah, but there is in ancient Greek texts. Nobody knows what or who the philosophers are referring to. The point is that the Church fathers felt compelled to incorporate Greek philosophy into Christianity. Socrates in his apology said: "O Athenians, You condemn me to death, me who I tried to wake you from the sleep of darkness. You will sleep until God takes pity on you and sends to you the one who will really wake you up. " (Plato, Apology of Socrates, 31 A).

Even more prophetic was Plato, who, among other things, announced the "crucifixion" of Christ. In the laws of Plato, he wrote "The righteous without being wronged will be flogged, beaten and finally crucified. According to Clement, Plato was even more prophetic in his book "Plato's Republic". In a dialogue between Socrates and Glaucon. Glaucon assumes that whereas most people have a blend of righteousness and unrighteousness in us, there would arise a man who will be totally unrighteous, and another man who will be totally righteous.

"For if he is going to be thought just he will have honors and gifts because of that esteem. We cannot be sure in that case whether he is just for sake of justice or for the sake of the gifts and the honors. So we must strip him bare of everything but justice and make his state the opposite of his imagined counterpart. Though doing no wrong he must

have the repute of the greatest injustice, so that he may be put to the test as regards justice through not softening because of ill repute and the consequences thereof. But let him hold on his course unchangeable even unto death seeming all his life to be unjust though being just, that so, both men attaining to the limit, the one of injustice, the other of justice, we may pass judgement which of the two is the happier (εὐδαιμονέστερος). ...

What [those who commend injustice] will say is this: that such being his disposition the just man will have to endure the lash, the rack, chains the branding-iron in his eyes, and finally, after every extremity of suffering, he will be impaled, and so will learn his lesson that not to be but to seem just is what we ought to desire" (Republic II.361b, 361e).

These prophecies can be a divine inspiration or just a coincidence, but the point here is the need for Church fathers to integrate Greek philosophy into Christianity. The Greek philosophy was seen by the Church Fathers as a true preparation for the Gospels. Specifically, the Platonic philosophy helped set the intellectual stage for the early church. Platonism, Aristotelianism, Cynicism, and Stoicism are parts of the essential form of Christian theology. As I said many times, you can see many similarities between Socrates' story and Jesus'. Both of them were sentenced to death for their teachings. There is also a small orthodox church in Greece dedicated to Saint Socrates.

Hesychasm the Meditation Practice
of the Orthodox Church:

Hesychasm is the invincible rock of the monastic life and theology. He who has not purified his mind through silence cannot reach the Divine. Orthodox Hesychasm gives major importance to the purity of the mind, which is the eye of the soul. The human mind is healthy when it is completely free from the thoughts of the sensible world. The idea of Hesychasm comes from Plato and Aristotle, and I have already mentioned that the influences of Plato on meditation practices derive from Socrates and the Pythagoreans. It's all about the substance and energy of God. The substance is reminiscent of the Platonic idea of the good and its identification with the divine, as something inconceivable to the human mind. Energy, on the other hand, is understood by the Aristotelian concept of motion and God: *The unmoved mover*.

The Book of Revelation and the Erythraean Sibyl:

Many ancient and modern interpreters report that the authorship of Revelation is a controversial issue and agree that the gospel of John and Revelation do not share the same author. The confusion occurs because the Book of Revelation is signed by a person called John. Revelation is distinct in many ways from the style of John's other writings. After all, many scholars found that the Roman emperor Domitian plunged John into boiling oil to death. Many Church Fathers agree that the Book of Revelation was not written by any of the apostles, nor even one of the saints and that this book is a heretic. The history of

Johannine authorship indicates that Revelation has been written before the Gospel. In ancient times the word Sibyl was used to describe any woman associated with the art of divination. Sibyl, therefore, means the one who reveals the will of God. The oracles of the Sibyls were guarded by ten armed men in the temple of Zeus at the Capitol of Rome. Unfortunately, some Sibylline texts were forged by Jews and Christians and used for promoting Christianity. So we are not sure about the authenticity of all the Sibylline texts. The prophecy of the Sibyl of Eritrea about the Second Coming of the Great King, it's by some Christian scholars authentic. The first person to save and publicly proclaim this oracle was Constantine the "Great"! Constantine admits that Erythraean Sibyl prophesied with the help of the god Apollo. So it was not Sibylla who prophesied, but Apollo himself! Although this important prophecy was proclaimed by Constantine, it was later set aside and silenced by the church. Because there was a danger of overturning the belief that the ancient Greek religion was a religion of demon worship. The prophecy begins with reference to the day of the Last Judgment, the day on which "the future king of the ages will descend from heaven" to judge all people without exception. Apart from the Gospel of Matthew, the similarities between the prophecy of Eritrea and the Revelation of John are striking:

"The light of day, the glow of the sun and the stars will disappear." (***Erythraean Sibyl***,)

"Trumpets from heaven, and a voice with great sorrow will be heard." (***Erythraean Sibyl***,)

"A fiery river will flow from the sky, and in fact from sulfur." (***Erythraean Sibyl***)

The most important common point between the Revelation of John and the prophecy of Erythraean is the reference to the famous "sign" that people will receive, which John calls "mark", while Eritrea "official seal"!

"Then there will be a sign in all people, an official seal." (***Erythraean Sibyl***).

Alexander's Gate, Gog and Magog, and the Inclosed Nations:

According to the Quran Isa shall come again to fight Gog and Magog and Al-Masih ad-Dajjal "False Messiah" and bring justice on earth. The legend of Gog and Magog and the Iron Gates of Alexander the Great was spread throughout the Near East in the early centuries of the Christian and Islamic eras. Gog and Magog were allies of Satan and kings of the Unclean Nations as described in the Book of Revelation, in Quran, in Visio Danielis text of St. John Chrysostom, and in a prophetic text of Saint Andrew. Alexander drove them beyond a mountain and lock them in the iron gates.

Pythagoreans and the Resurrection Initiation:

Christians tell us that Jesus descended to Hades and after his death was resurrected on the third day. But did you know that resurrection was a part of initiation into the Pythagorean mysteries? We have so many Resurrections in Pythagorean history, the most known is that of Pythagoras in Italy. The great painting of Salvator Rosa - *The secret of resurrection* (1662), is not about the Resurrection of Jesus, but the painting depicted Pythagoras emerging from the underworld. "You can research online for this beautiful painting," Hieronymus said that when Pythagoras went down into Hades he saw Hesiod and Homer punished for the things they said about the gods. In Italy, Pythagoras wanted to prove the immortality of the soul. For that reason, he dug a grave and went inside for a few days. When everyone thought that Pythagoras was dead, he came out of the tomb weak and emaciated but revealed that the soul is immortal. Zalmoxis was a student of Pythagoras and a founder of a mystical cult in the Thracian region. According to Plato, Zalmoxis was a physician and a great healer of the body and soul (psyche).

Zalmoxis died and was resurrected like Jesus. This was defended also by Jean (Ioan) Coman, a professor of patristics and Orthodox priest. Zalmoxis withdrew for three years in a natural cave on the holy Kogaionon mountain of Romania and was considered dead, but after three years, he was resurrected and come back from Hades.

Seneca tells the story of Julius Canus, a philosopher who was initiated into the Pythagorean mysteries. He informed his disciples that he will reappear three days after his death. As he promised, he returned from the tomb and appeared to his disciples three days after his death.

Jesus' teaching resembles that of Stoics, Cynics, and Socrates

Socrates is the main influence on Cynic philosophy. The similarities between Socrates and Jesus are obvious but what about the Stoics and Cynics? The Cynics were an important Greek philosophical school that was founded about the time of Alexander the Great. The main goal of Cynic philosophy is the liberation from desire, and the achievement of virtue, and morality. Many scholars including Burton L. Mack and John Dominic Crossan suggested that Jesus has been influenced by Cynicism. Here are some examples:

Matthew 10:10:
"Do not carry a traveler's bag with a change of clothes and sandals or even a walking stick" (like cynics).

Matthew 6:34

Matthew 6:34

"Therefore do not worry about tomorrow, for tomorrow will worry about itself. Each day has enough trouble of its own." Therefore I tell you, do not worry about your life, what you will eat or drink; or about your body, what you will wear. Is not life more than food, and the body more than clothes? Look at the birds of the air; they do not sow or reap or store away in barns, and yet your heavenly Father feeds them. Are you not much more valuable than they? Therefore do not worry about tomorrow, for tomorrow will worry about itself. Each day has enough trouble of its own.

The German professor J. Leipoldt once wrote, "*Jesus Christ, by elevating his love of neighbor to the highest moral standards, rejected any Jewish custom which was unethical, while being closer to Greek thought, especially to the Greek Stoicism.*"

Hypatia of Alexandria:

Hypatia of Alexandria is one of the many examples of Plagiarism by early Christians. Hypatia was a Greek Neoplatonic philosopher, mathematician, and astronomer, who lived in Alexandria of Egypt. Hypatia was accused of using witchcraft by Christian zealots led by Peter the Lector. First, they dragged her into a church, where they undressed her and beat her to death with roofing tiles and later they tore her body apart and burned it. Hypatia was incorporated as a symbol of Christianity and scholars believe she was part of the basis for the legend of Saint Catherine of Alexandria.

Saint Nektarios on Greek Philosophy:

Greek philosophy is the foundation of true growth and education. It is the human teacher and the road map to godliness. Is the teacher of truth, teaching humans about their true identity and purpose in the world, as well as the existence of God, their relationship with God, and God's relationship with humans. Greek philosophy demonstrated God's providence for humanity through its excellent theories and evolved into a teacher of humanity in Christ. - **Saint Nektarios**.

There is light and darkness everywhere. As we can see, there were both religious exploiters and spiritual people in Christianity. What we need to do is to keep only what is pure and discard what is not.

Philosophy and Pangratium:

The Ancient Greek Pankration was the first multi-art fighting system (MMA). It was a combination of wrestling, kicks, and boxing without straps. That's why Pankration is also called the mother of martial arts. This mixed martial art is said to have begun with Theseus, and Hercules. With the crusades of Alexander the Great, Pankration spread to India. It is believed that Pankration is the ancestor of all Asian martial arts. The holistic martial art of Pankration was the favorite sport of the ancient philosophers. Pythagoras, Socrates, Aristotle, and even the father of medicine Hippocrates were Pancratists. Plato was Pancratist and also a wrestler. In fact, he was a three-time champion, with one victory in Pankration and two in wrestling. His real name was Aristocles and not Plato. They called him Plato (πλατυς- wide) because he was wide on the chest. The word pankration is compounded by (Pan) which means everything and (Krato) which means I hold. Pankration = I hold everything. Zeus was called Zeus Pagratis, meaning Almighty. The historian Philostratus describes Pankration as "the best of Olympic games" «των εν Ολυμπία το κάλλιστον».

Now, what's the reason that the ancient philosophers loved Pankration? Simply, like MMA and any other martial art, Pankration has a lot of mental benefits like discipline, focus, increased confidence, etc, but besides that, a combat sport like Pankration is like a chess match and works as a perfect counterbalance of Philosophy. "Mens sana in corpore sano." A sound mind in a sound body. Pankration was one of the main rules of Pythagoreans. Pythagoreans had to be vegetarians, train in Pankration, and were required to observe periods of silence. Marcus Aurelius said: "All sports entertain, the pancratium produces wisdom." The famous Japanese karate masters Tatsuo Suzuki, Hirokazu Kanazawa, and Masutasu Oyama (Mas Oyama) who is also the founder of Kyokushin Karate had always supported the idea that Karate began in Ancient Greece and not in Japan and that came to Asia with the invasion of Alexander the Great.

Pankration in Asia and Bodhidharma:

Pankration is about 2000 years old, and as I mentioned before some scholars agree that with Alexander the Great this martial art spread to the far East. Greek Buddhism (Greco-Buddhism) began in the 4th century BC. with the beginning of the Hellenistic period and continued until the 5th century BC. Bodhidharma was a legendary Buddhist monk who lived during the 5th century. His name means "dharma of awakening" in Sanskrit. Alexander founded various cities in Bactria, such as Alexandria of the Oxus (Ai-Khanoum) and Alexandria of the Caucasus (Bagram).

Bodhidharma, the father of Shaolin Kung-Fu and founder of Zen Buddhism was described as a Bactrian Buddhist monk. Buddhist art depicts Bodhidharma as a barbaric Caucasian with Blue-eyes (ì 胡: Bìyǎn hú Chinese texts). The Hellenobactrians conquered parts of northern India in 180 BC and they were known as Indo-Greeks. They controlled various areas of northern India until 10 AD. Pankration influenced Shaolin Kung Fu especially in the province of Yunnan (Yunnan = Ionian = Greece,) and consequently the Japanese martial arts. Here are some quotes by my favorite philosopher, Socrates.

"No man has the right to be an amateur in the matter of physical training. It is a shame for a man to grow old without seeing the beauty and strength of which his body is capable." — Socrates.

"Exercise is superior to medicine because it is better to be healthy, than try to regain your health later." — Socrates.

"When our bodies become soft our souls lose their power too" – Socrates.

Pygmachia – Ancient Pugilism:

Boxing is one of my favorite combat sports. Today is used by many as a self-defense sport and as a good way to lose weight and gain muscles. A long time ago this sport was completely different and here is why. Boxing, (pugilism) has roots that go back to ancient Greece and Rome. There is clear evidence that boxing existed on Crete Island as early as 1500 BC. An Ancient Greek form of boxing known as Pygmachia (fistfight) was featured in all of the Panhellenic festivals and of course in the Olympics. Fighters were fighting without gloves but with leather taped onto their hands. Pygmachia was thought to cultivate courage, endurance, pain tolerance, and help the citizens of Athens in difficult situations. For that reason, boxing was one of the main exercises in the military for young people. In boxing philosophy, there was a clear distinction between physical violence and the injury of an athlete. Plato believed that fighters had to be always calm and achieve modesty and lack of vanity. Aristotle considered the athletes of boxing equal to the poets and musicians and characterized them as good and honest. Aristophanes states that the heroes of Marathon grew up in pavilions and gyms. Plutarch believed that the three sports – boxing, wrestling, and pankration were warfare. Boxing in ancient Greece was tougher than today's professional boxing. In ancient boxing, there were no weight classes, no rounds with intermediate breaks, no points, no victory or defeat at the points, and no stoppage in the event of hemorrhage of the athletes. The winner was the one who would knock out the opponent or force him to abandon the fight. In the case of a long race with no winner, the terrible Climax "κλίμαξ" was applied, with the agreement of both opponents. Each of the opponents accepted a beating on the face, without making any move to avoid it until one of the two is knocked out!

Sacred Healing:

Sacred healing and ancient Greek secrets about health.
Legends, myths, beliefs, and healing arts.

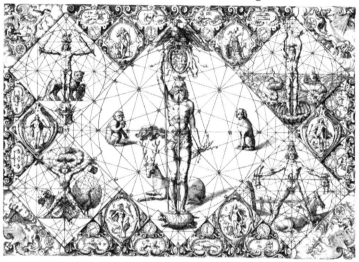

Genesis and Greek Mythology:

ncient Greek mythology has many similarities with Genesis. Genesis describes the same events as ancient Greeks. Probably there is a universal pre-history here. The Titans and Giants of ancient Greece and the Giants (Nephilim) of Genesis. Deucalion and Noah (Deucalion, is the Greek equivalent of Noah) and so on... Here are two of the most important.

Angels and Demons in Ancient Greece:

Initially in epic poetry Demons were called Gods. Also, in the word Demon, they attributed the meaning of the guardian angel. In ancient Greece, demons played an important role in human life. They are found in many ancient Greek books, such as those of Homer, Hesiod, Plato, Plutarch, Herodotus, etc. They are mainly referred to as Deities acting in the heavenly space between Gods and humans. They are in a sense the intermediary messengers of the Gods to the earthly realm, and vice versa, because their relationship is reciprocal. After Hesiod, philosophers such as Aristotle and Plato wrote that the Demons are "children of Gods" while they were characterized either as fate-bearing of good or bad depending on their character, "good-daimons or bad-daimons." Let's don't forget also the famous Socrates daemon, that through his daemon he made the correct decisions.

The Garden of Eden and the Hesperides:

Again here Ancient Greek mythology has similarities with Genesis. Genesis describes Adam and Eve in the garden of Eden and the Greek religious texts describe the Garden of the Hesperides that was the home of Zeus and Hera, in which there was a grove of citrus fruits and golden apple trees. The big difference is that the serpent in Greek mythology enlightened, and not deceived Zeus and Hera in the garden. Many scholars locate both, the garden of Eden and the Garden of the Hesperides in Africa.

What this chapter has to do with wellness? Another commonality of Greek mythology and Genesis is that Hesperides and the Garden of Eden are described as places of absolute well-being. Clearly, if the early chapters of the Book of Genesis and the stories of Hesperides in Greek mythology present a true account of human origins, then we have an original testimony that the first humans were fruitarians. Arnold Ehret, a German naturopath and alternative health educator, claimed that "The Garden of Eden was a garden of fruit trees. That means that man, for thousands of years, through a wrong culture, has been deceived into an unconscious suicide, becoming a slave and produces the wrong unnatural foods that cause disease and death." Dr. Walker is absolutely certain that the first humans until relatively recently were entirely fruit-eaters. The findings of these claims were reported in detail on May 15, 1979, in the New York Times, with the title: Research yields surprises about early human diets. The importance of Walker's research is that although humans have adopted omnivorous and carnivorous eating practices, our anatomy and physiology have not changed. We remain organically a species of a fruit diet.

Fate Destiny and Karma:

The terms fate and destiny are often used as the same thing. So, what is the difference between fate, destiny, and karma? Many wise people think that you create your fate, but your destiny is sealed. Now, the question is, we are masters of our fate and we step on a path to a predetermined destiny, or we can change it? I think the answer is a little bit of both. Destiny (destination) is where you end up and fate is how you end up there. Everyone shapes their fate and destiny is what we become in the end. Karma has nothing to do with destiny or fate. Karma is one of the factors that influence this course. We are all responsible for our karma. In ancient Greece, karma was called Antipeponthos "equivalent exchange." The word Antipeponthos comes from the words instead and suffer and it has the meaning: "Suffer from the consequences of actions". Karma is a Sanskrit word that roughly translates to "action." Every action has consequences.

Can we "Burn" the Bad Karma?

Karma is about the nature of our intentions. Each action a person takes, good or bad, will affect him or her in the future. Whatever we throw away to the sky is what comes back to us. However, the point is, can we change our karma? The answer is Yes. We can't stop our karma but we can change it. With the practice of morality and compassion, we can change it! Check your intentions, love and forgive, be honest, choose to be positive when things are difficult, change your actions, and release your judgment about yourself and others, so that you can calmly explore your karma. In Jainism, fasting together with ethics used as a technique that burns bad karma. Fasting practiced along with meditation and Self-study has a great power to discipline the mind. Karma in modern science is Newton's third law: For every action, there is an equal and opposite reaction. The law of action and reaction. "Cause and effect." "Every action has an equal reaction".

The Healing Powers and Meaning of Dreams in Ancient Times:

From ancient times many people tried to understand the mechanism of dreams (oneiromancy). Even today, dreams are inexplicable and supernatural. Many of us had a dream that we didn't give attention to it, but a week later we saw the exact dream we had or just scenes from the dream in real life. Why do some dreams come true and are so accurate? These precognitive dreams it's happened to most people at least once. In the Christian, Hindu, and Muslim religions, dreams are part of communication with God. In Ancient Egypt and Greece, people believed that dreams are an innate gift. Actually, for Ancient Greeks, dreams were oracles, bringing messages from the Gods. The ancient Egyptians and Assyrians were the first who write dream books around 2000-1500 BC.

Dreams in Greek Mythology:

In Greek mythology, sleep was a demon and was the son of Night and Erebus (darkness). He and his twin brother, Death, were living in Tartarus. According to ancient Greeks, sleep lives on the Island of Dreams. In the middle of the dream island is the oblivion lake. Residents of the island are the dreams "Oneiroi". There are two gates on the Island of Dreams: the Gates of Horn and Ivory. The false dreams "not all dreams are prophetic" depart from the Ivory gate and the true dreams from the Horn gate. The three main sons of sleep rule the realm of dreams: Morpheus, Phobetor, and Phantasos 'Fantasy'. Fasting played an important role in oneiromancy and in the process of precognitive dreams. Oneiromancy comes from the Gods and can't be taught. Both brothers, eternal death, and temporary sleep can guide us to the truth and enlightenment. Both daughters of Apollo, medicine, and divination are related. As I mentioned before Asclepius the supreme physician was the son of Apollo too. Therapeutic sleepiness was practiced in Asclepius treatment centers. The patient had to sleep in a sacred place to receive a revealing dream for therapeutic purposes. According to Orpheus and Plato, sleep is where the study of death begins. In conclusion, philosophy has the same results as sleep, the awakening from the illusion, (philosophical death).

"When we sleep, we do not know if we are men or women, the soul is immutable, as is the Divine." **Yogi Sri Yukteswar**.

Artemidorus Oneirocritica:

Oneirocritica (Ονειροκριτικά) was written and digested into five books by the ancient philosopher Artemidorus in the 2nd century AD. It's an ancient Greek treatise on dream interpretation. Artemidorus collected all this material while traveling to mainland Greece, the Greek islands, and Italy, where he searched for popular gatherings and celebrations, the wisdom perpetuated by popular tradition with examples and explanations. Carl Gustav Jung and Freud were greatly influenced by Artemidorus. Jung believed in the quality of dreams that show the future, the divinatory dreams, and the universal habits of mankind. Freud, in his book Interpretation of Dreams, mentions Artemidorus eight times. Artemidorus tried to categorize dreams: First is the theoretical dreams which literally predict the future, and second are the allegorical or symbolic dreams, whose decipherment leads to the prediction of the future. It excludes dreams that are caused by physical or mental deprivation or intense desire. The entire ancient Greek literature is full of dream-loving references and attempts.

Native Americans Dream Healing:

Dream catchers are one of the most fascinating traditions of Native Americans. Dreamcatchers are used to assure that only positive dreams can pass through the hole, and negative dreams are caught in the webbing. Native Americans have practiced lucid dreaming techniques for centuries. Within the dreams, they experience prophecies and therapies. They look at the signs of a dream before hunting, fishing, or any other activity.

Astral Dream Travel:

People of this theory believe that we travel through a time continuum. With Astral dream travel, you can run faster through time and see the future. That doesn't mean that we travel in the future through dreams. It is more like we see what's coming. Like when you watch a football game in slow motion, you know when a player is going to shoot, just from his movements before. Early morning dreams are the easiest to remember. That happens because we are changing from the REM level, through the Theta Level. Theta level is used as a treatment for various diseases.

Subconscious Memories:

Deja Vu (some explain Deja Vu as trapped subconscious memories or predictions) and dreams can predict the future. Some say that people with double Temporal Lobe Epilepsy can see into the future, but it is not proven yet.

Our Brains are Powerful:

In my opinion, dreams are a mix of subconscious predictions and human instinct (sixth sense or third eye). Dreams also provide help for solving day emotional problems. Our mind stores information while we sleep and things that were too stressful to deal with throughout the day are handled in a less threatening environment.

Music Therapy and Frequencies Healing:

One thing that all cultures have in common is music. Music was not invented by man but given to him by god. It's our universal language and a powerful tool for healing. Here is a famous Nikola Tesla quote "If you want to find the secrets of the universe, think in terms of energy, frequency, and vibration." The Greek philosopher Pythagoras prescribed music as medicine. Healers and shamans play the drums and sing for healing purposes. Researchers believe that shaman music can open the subconscious of the patients. Music is also called the "language of the soul" and according to some new studies, music can lower blood pressure and is good for the heart. The combination of music and physical exercise triggers the release of endorphins that have many health benefits including alleviating depression, reducing stress, and anxiety.

Music therapy is very beneficial. According to a study in the Netherlands, creative thinking can be enhanced through music. The biggest problem of modern society is the lack of harmony. Another piece of evidence that music can work as medicine is some studies on plants. Many studies have shown that playing music to plants promotes faster and healthier growth. Jazz and classical music appear to have more beneficial effects, but even rock, country, pop, etc. have similar effects. The grandeur of music lies behind and beyond sounds, in Silence. Pythagoras had reached this level of "sensitivity" to hear (not of course with the ears) the symphony of heaven, the music of the spheres. For Pythagoras and his students, harmony begins within the man himself, in his soul. Plato also talks about the importance of music to young people, as rhythm and harmony penetrate the soul and can bring positive or disastrous effects on their character. He suggested that young people must be trained in gymnastics and learn music. Exercise for the body and music for the soul. According to the Ancient Greek legends Orpheus, enchanted with his music not only humans but also beasts. Wild beasts came out of their nests and stood at his feet. Trees and even rocks moved near so they can hear his melodies. The harmony of music can affect all beings.

The Healing Power of Sound Frequencies:

Frequency is waves caused by the vibration speed. For example, a 432Hz Frequency is 432 waves per second.

432Hz:

According to research, 432 Hz is more friendly for the ears and has healing powers. It is often called the frequency of the universe as it helps with anxiety and brings down the heart rate and blood pressure. The ancient Egyptian and Greek instruments were tuned to A=432 Hz. Conspiracy theories suggest, that the change from 432Hz to 440 Hz frequency was deliberately adopted by governments for manipulating the masses. Another theory suggested, that the Nazis changed 432Hz to 440 Hz to spread fear and control the masses.

528hz:

Known as the love frequency. 528 hz can repair DNA and prevent illnesses and disorders.

396Hz:

396Hz boosts your inner peace, cleans the feeling of guilt and fear, and builds a strong magnetic field of positive energy.

417Hz:

It helps you focus, removes negative energy from the body, and heals the sacral chakra.

639Hz:

Is the vibration of the Heart Chakra. Good for communication and creation. Finally, it brings harmony and love.

741Hz:

This is the frequency of Throat Chakra, it cleans negativity, anger, and even toxins.

852Hz:

It helps with inner strength and peace, expands awareness and spiritualism.

963Hz:

It opens your mind as is associated with Pineal Gland Activation (Third Eye) and with Crown Chakra.

18Hz:

18 Hz is said to produce hallucinations or paranormal sightings. It is also called the Ghost frequency. I add this frequency just to show how powerful frequencies are. We still don't know if 18hz sound causes humans to experience hallucinations or opens a gate to real paranormal activity.

The Health Benefits of Grounding (Earthing):

Earthing is contact with the Earth's surface electrons by walking barefoot, but is Earthing a therapeutic ancient technique or just a hoax? One theory of Earthing is that humans are lacking electrons because shoes prevent the free flow of electrons and that walking Barefoot can get them back to the connection with mother Earth. It sounds stupid right? Wrong. The first time that I saw the earthing grounding was from a survival instructor (Cody Lundin) in the dual survival documentary series. Serious studies have revealed that electrically grounding produces intriguing effects on health. Grounding can be a viable complementary natural therapy. But let's have a look first at some Earthing grounding benefits:

Earthing Grounding Benefits:
Grounding Helps the Immune System.
It is very beneficial for Wound Healing.
It Helps with Chronic Inflammation and Autoimmune Diseases.
Reduces Stress Levels.
Improves Circulation.
Earthing Grounding Prevents Insomnia.
Reduces the Chance of Osteoporosis.
Increases Energy.
It Reduces the Risk of Cardiovascular Disease.
Reduces Pain.

Another way to understand this besides studies is by logic. When we walk barefoot on a beach with beautiful sand or in a forest, we feel amazing and we have a sense of freedom. Other benefits of walking barefoot include improvements in balance, relaxation, and a free foot Massage which can work as reflexology (Reflexology helps with back pain, neck pain, stiffness, shoulder tension, headache, toothache, etc.) Many philosophers walked barefoot, perhaps that was one of the reasons that they were so wise.

Earth Ley Lines and Ancient Monuments:

L ey lines or earth Chakras are alignments of several places of geographical and historical interest, such as ancient monuments! Sacred sites like the Egyptian Pyramids, Peru's Machu Picchu, Stonehenge, the Great Wall of China, and so on… Almost all historical sites seem to have been built in a perfectly straight line. These lines connect both natural and sacred prehistoric structures. Most cultures have traditions and words to describe the lines. Chinese for example, called them the Dragon lines. Some people think that are Portals or energetically charged points. The phrase (ley line) was coined by the amateur archaeologist Alfred Watkins, in 1921. Referring to alignments of numerous places of geographical and historical interest!

Earth Geophysical Powers:

Are these "Energy Chakras" surrounding the planet real, or is it just fiction? We know that the human body has Chakras, but what about mother earth? Scientists can not understand why these alignments exist and energies cannot be detected by any scientific device, but as I mentioned above, Nikola Tesla said: "If you want to find the secrets of the universe, think in terms of energy, frequency, and vibration." Although earth ley lines are invisible to us, ancient civilizations sensed the power of the earth and built their monuments there. In my opinion, our ancient ancestors would never have erected a monument if the location was not sacred (charged with energy) or filled with paranormal activity. If Earth ley lines exist, that explains a lot about the Chinese term Feng Shui. Today, they are many documentaries about the geophysical powers of Ancient monuments. Built or placed in specific parts of the world, to pump energy flows of the Earth. Something like Acupuncture.

Trees Healing Properties and Powers:

I've always been fascinated by ancient trees due to their unquestionably healing properties. Sacred trees are found in almost every ancient folklore of the world. In ancient times, the trees were the divine wisdom keepers of the Earth. Many people including me, walk through forests and meditate under those trees, so they can connect with their energy. In India, sacred trees are visited by people seeking blessings for health and fertility. Sacred Trees are like antennas of cosmic vibration and they can help you to connect with Mother Earth.

Sacred Trees List:

Almond tree.
Oaktree.
Ash tree
Sacred Marula tree of Africa.
The Magnolia tree.
Tea tree and eucalyptus of the Australian Aborigines.
Pine Tree.
Walnut tree.
White Willow tree.
Fig tree.

A tree deity (tree spirit) is a nature deity related to a tree. These kinds of deities are present in many cultures. In ancient Greece, Dryads and Amadryades were nymphs of the forests. They were born and grown within oak trees and other spiritual trees.

When a tree was cut, the nymph moved to another tree and punished the one who cut the tree. The Dryads were nymphs of the forests, while Amadryades were associated with trees.

List of Tree Deities Worldwide:
Dryads, hamadryads, and Meliae (Ash tree) in Greece.
Hathor, Egypt.
Kodama and Kurozome, Japan.
Nang Ta-khian (Ta-khian tree) and Nang Tani (wild banana tree) in Thailand.
Penghou, (a dog-shaped spirit) and Pi-Fang in China.
Rakapila of Madagascar.

The Philosophy and Therapeutic Powers of the Druids:

Druids were known as mystics and scholars of natural law. Some say that Druids had a strong connection with the Greeks. According to Roman historiography, the oak tree was also the sacred tree of the Greek royal houses of Macedonia. The word Druid is derived from the Greek word δρυς= oak. Extensive references are made by Greek and Roman writers. Posidonius of Rhodes, a Greek Stoic philosopher who studied the Celts, appreciated Druids as philosophers, saying, "Even the barbarian race gave their place to wisdom." The French word druiah means "wise man." Generally, Druid in Celtic tradition meant "wise man of the tree". The teachings of the Druids were very similar to those of Pythagoras. They taught the existence of a future state of rewards and punishment, the immortality of the soul, and reincarnation. The deepest secrets of the doctrine were known only to the initiated who received the nomination after 20 years of training and study. Folklore, always tend to exaggerate, but through reports, we can conclude that druids were excellent healers and they knew many secrets of nature. They had also amazing abilities and used the physical environment for coverage. Druids observed natural phenomena to predict the weather. Almost nothing else is known about the religious worship of Druids other than the ritual of oak and mistletoe as described by Pliny the Elder. As the mistletoe was considered sacred, it was collected from oaks with a golden scythe on a certain day of the year and after collecting it, they sacrificed two white bulls.

Healing Crystals and Healing Stones:

Crystal healing is used as a natural medical technique for many diseases. This therapy is based on two main concepts, the chi or prana, and the chakras. But is crystal healing genuine? Can the crystal stones and gems use for therapeutic purposes? Many people claim that crystal healing is just pseudoscience. Some others state that crystal healing works, but only as a placebo, while others believe that crystal energy is an ancient secret knowledge for healing and power. To be honest, I would never have taken this treatment seriously if I hadn't discovered it by accident in the Ancient Orphic texts. Lithika 'Stones', was written by the ancient Greek Orpheus and it is the first known ancient script dealing with the healing and magical properties of the stones and their ritual practice. A study found that crystals have no healing powers and that is just the placebo effect that works, but believers claim that this study failed, as crystals may take weeks or even months to reach their full healing potential. A crystal does not have any effect on the user until it becomes "one" with a person's energy. Crystals also must discharge and charge before using them again. But, before you think that crystal healing is just a hoax, let me remind you of something very important. Scientific evidence showed that physical metals like gold, silver, platinum, and copper have antibacterial, anti-inflammatory, germicidal, and antimicrobial properties. Physical metals fight infections, help with wound healing, and so on. So, if metals have all these healing properties then why do crystal stones and gems that coming also from mother earth don't?

Another example is Aura. If you were talking about aura some years ago, they take you for a fool, but today with Kirlian photography we can see that human aura is real. The technique has been known as electrography. Kirlian thought that these images could be used to diagnose illnesses.

Crystal Powers and the Atlanteans:

Some people support the idea that we had an earlier civilization that used crystal technology for creating energy. Atlantis is said to be the first that had machines made of crystals. We all have watched TV movies and documentaries about the Atlanteans and the use of crystals. We all thought that those kinds of stories are myths, and perhaps they are, but crystals, such as quartz, can be tapped for electricity using a piezoelectric (mechanical energy discharge) method. By securing the crystal and subjecting it to direct force with a permanent magnet, a detectable amount of electricity is released. Some people go even deeper and build orgone pyramids. Orgonite is an energy healing device made from resin, metal, and crystals, known for its ability to convert negative energy into positive energy.

The Long-Lived Race of Hyperboreans:

This is a story of a race, blessed with longevity. HYPERBOREA (ΥΠΕΡΒΟΡΕΙΑ) was a mythical kingdom in the far North beyond the land of winter and had as its capital Thule. The Hyperborean Race (Ὑπερβόρεοι), was named after Boreas, a north wind and one of the four directional Anemoi (wind-gods). The Greek explorer Pytheas is the first to have written for Thule. Later the Greek historian Herodotus mentioned the Egyptian legend of the continent of Hyperborea in the far north. According to Greek and Roman legends, people there lived for thousands of years and had found the ultimate happiness. The sun in Hyperborean never goes down and the place was full of gold. People were blessed there, a long-lived race that has found the secret of youth! The Thule legend was also one of the main reasons that the second world war started. Hitler was a member of the Thule secret Society. A German occultist society of the Volkisch movement in Munich. Thule Gesellschaft and Vril Society were the forces that helped to bring the Führer into power. Thule and Vril Society believed also in Vril energy. Vril energy was the power of the Aryan race. The legend says that Hyperborea was older than Atlantis and Lemuria. For many is considered the gateway to other worlds and the opening to the Hollow Earth. Another Greek myth tells that Apollo migrates each December from Delphi to Hyperborea to return in the spring to Delos with his chariot drawn by swans. Theseus and Perseus also visited Hyperborea according to different legends.

From the time of Alexander the Great, maps depicted Hyperborea generally as a peninsula or an island beyond the territories of France. Some others connect Hyperborea with the Druids and Stonehenge. Probably most people imagine this kingdom in the territory of today Norway and Sweden. One of the most popular theories for the collapse of the Hyperborean race is the physical destruction of the earth's axis.

Abaris the Hyperborean:

Abaris was a healer, a prophet, and a priest of Apollo in the legendary land of Hyperborea. He is very important, as according to Herodotus and other historical and mythological sources including the Suda lexicon, this shamanistic figure left Hyperborea to save other nations from a plague pandemic and traveled around the world with an arrow that the god Apollo gave him. Plato considered him one of the best Thracian-Scythian physicians who practice medicine upon the body and soul. In Iamblichus's Vita Pythagorica is said that Abaris purified the plague from numerous cities, including Knossos and Sparta. During my research, I was fascinated when I discovered that the Hyperborean race lived in forests and they were fruitarians. In ancient Mythology, it is mentioned that these people "did not have any diseases and lived for a long time". Abaris in Greek means weightless-lightweight. That probably means that Abaris was really lean. During his visit to Greece, no one saw him eating or drinking.

That's another amazing fact, as Abaris probably fasted for long periods or he was a breatharian. When Avaris arrived in Greece, he renewed his friendship with the Delian Greeks. According to the Neoplatonists and the De Vita Pythagorica "On the Pythagorean life", Avaris approached Pythagoras in Italy to learn Greek philosophy. Pythagoras did not apply the pedagogical method of the five-year silence and the other trials, but in a short time, he taught him the books "On Nature" and "On the Gods".

The Fountain of Youth and the Ambrosia Elixir:

The biggest fear of humans is death. The quest for a way to remain young forever has become a part of human history in legends like the Fountain of Youth, the tree of Life, the Abrosia of the Gods, and of course the Soma Elixir.

The Fountain of Youth:

Alexander the Great, King Prester John, and the famous explorer Juan Ponce de Leon are only some of the people that tried to find the fountain of youth. Alexander the Great crossed the Land of Darkness in his search for the Water of Life. King Prester John, ruled a land containing a similar fountain during the early Crusades in the 11th and 12th centuries AD. Finally, the Fountain of youth was said to have been found in the New World (Bimini), by Ponce de Leon. For many years, explorers organized expeditions to places such as Shambhala, among the mountains of the Himalayas, where it is said that the secrets of eternal youth were hidden. At the moment, there is not any evidence to support that the fountain of youth was or it is real. Unfortunately, we do not have any documents from Ponce de Leon's mission to Florida. The source of youth was never discovered.

Soma Abrosia the Elixir of Immortality:

Soma in Ancient India was the drink of Gods, was a panacea, and was the secret elixir of immortality. It was not only a sacred drink but also a sacred deity (energy). The identity of the ancient Soma is one of the greatest mysteries. There has been a long search for the identity of the original Soma plant. The plant was called soma by the Indian and haoma by the Iranians. Many of the westerner scholars believe that the Soma plant was perhaps Ephedra, cannabis, ginseng, opium, or, even the fly-agaric mushroom (which was used by many shamans, but the Soma plant was described with leaves, which mushrooms do not have). Both cannabis and Ephedra had been used in conjunction with the making of hallucinogenic drinks. In ancient times, the worshipper who knew how to make Soma will gain power like those of Indian deities. Drinking Soma produces immortality. Amrita is a Sanskrit word that literally means "immortality" and is phonetically and conceptually similar to the Greek ambrosia. Ambrosia in ancient Greece was the drink of the Gods. I find this fascinating, as two different groups of ancient deities need the same drink to gain power. The Rigveda describes Soma as a plant that grows near the water. Finally, Soma was also connected to the practice of alchemy and the philosopher's stone.

Evexiandros Quotes and a Summary Wellness Guide:

Before closing, it is a good idea to summarize the texts in a wellness guide. In this chapter, I will attempt to bring together ideas from ancient philosophy as well as my own philosophical views and quotes. So, what have we learned so far about on wellness philosophy handbook?

On the one hand, we have the flow of the mutable materials of the world of Heraclitus and on the other the immutable of Parmenides. Plato spoke about the theory of Forms which is immutable, unborn, incorruptible and reflects on our mutable world. But also Aristotle had written about the first Unmoved mover in his book "Metaphysics". The Indian sages of yoga have taught us about the Maya concept which is the delusion that does not allow us to see beyond dualism. Maya exists because people can not grasp anything beyond the three dimensions. But, in my opinion, this does not imply that the immutable, immortal, and incorruptible do not exist in our world, but rather that we do not perceive it.

As Apollonius Tyaneus once said:

"*Death does not exist for anyone, except apparently, nor does birth exist for anyone, except apparently. The change of essence into nature is considered birth, while the change of nature into essence is considered death. Nothing is truly born or ever worn out, only one becomes visible and then invisible. Everything changes into parts, and parts into the whole due to the unity of everything*"

Now, the important thing for me is that while many philosophers had referred to immortal, unborn, immovable, immutable, and so on, they haven't explained or understood that all of these terms are also associated with dualism. What they called on Ancient Greece Bliss and in India Nirvana is the fine line of balance between mutable and immutable. The term <u>unit</u> that many philosophers use to explain the Divine can be found for me in the balance of dualism which leads to the Human perfection. Death occurs when the soul enters the world of the immutable and awaits rebirth in the world of the mutable until it reaches final realization, the EUDEMONIA (the balance of dualism).

My Quotes and Rules of Wellness:

"Wellness is the balance of body, soul and spirit."

"Wellness is the only path to bliss."

A virtuousness-well-being combination is the best way to eudaimonia."

"Only through balance and the middle way we achieve wellness."

"Imbalance can cause mental and physical symptoms which can lead to a disease."

"All things have their golden mean."

"We need to find the golden mean within ourselves and the golden mean in the things and situations we get involved."

"Practice and make the middle way your second nature".

"We need the extremes and we have to find balance in the extremes."

"Extremes force our bodies to adapt and become stronger".

"With extremes balance increases."

"Only balanced pleasure can lead to well-being."

"The Divine cannot be defined but can be known."

"Divine, it's all and nothing, whole but empty, one and many."

"Atheist, agnostic or theist they are all right, as the Divine it's all and nothing."

"The ultimate goal of our existence is the perfection and union with the Divine."

"The only way to achieve bliss (eudaimonia) is by the wellness-middle path."

"Through wellness we can have small connections of bliss in our daily lives."

"The more we are connected with the Divine through our inner highest part of the soul, the more likely we are to achieve eudaimonia after death."

"The inner highest part of the soul is like duplicating Carbon that copies our experiences for a final exam."

"Use exercise for the body, philosophy for the mind, and meditation for the soul."

"Use a mix of Epicureanism and Stoicism in your daily life."

"Although I am a lover of pleasure and I have lived a hedonistic life as moderate pleasure is a form of well-being. Now that I m older I realized that the greatest pleasure is self-sufficiency. Through discipline you acquire self-sufficiency, which is the supreme pleasure. But keep in mind, if you do not get enough pleasures when younger you will not be ready for self-sufficiency ".

Evexiandros More Quotes:

"Philosophy is the best cure for the soul."

"Those who philosophize in modern times are like flowers among thorns."

"We must bring the body the mind and soul into harmony."

"Moderation is best in all things, goodness is moderation and has nothing to do with the self-pity of Christianity."

"Great minds cannot create something good today because everything is rejected by the false experts."

"Morality is the greatest well-being."

"I can say for sure that I am a philosopher because fortunately, philosophy is for everyone, No need for fake experts with pseudo-titles."

"My travels are my dowry."

"Experiences nurture the soul."

"Goodness is the medicine of the soul. You give it to others but you benefit the most."

"Health is just part of Wellness."

"The ancient quote 'Moderation is Best' is more clear as 'Moderation is Bliss.'"

"Jealousy is the brother of madness."

"Today sex is overrated, people that ask you inappropriate questions like when was the last time you had sex is because they didn't have enough in their lives."

"Correct thinking cannot arise from fear."

"People pretend to care about moral values, but when difficult times come, they easily betray the values of life."

"Enough with the darkness of religions and the deception of modern pseudoscience. Science tells us not to believe in the supernatural while also claiming that our senses deceive us."

"Philosophy is soul medicine"
"There are two kinds of realities or truths. The truth from the senses and the philosophical truth. Only philosophical truth is correct. We can't always rely on our senses because they can deceive us. As an example, I will use love. People who are in love trust their feelings and senses and are unable to see their lover's true character. "Love can blind you" or better "senses can blind you". Only philosophical truth can lead us to philosophical death. The philosophical death is the rebirth of human."

"Fanaticism is dangerous. Any political spectrum Left-wing or right-wing it's wrong. Like, if you hold ice in your hands for more than 2 minutes instead of being frozen, it burns like fire. Cold and Hot become the same if you think in extremes."

"Authority corrupts the human spirit."

Please Consider Leaving a Review:

Writing a book takes a lot of time and effort. If you enjoyed this book and feel that you gained knowledge regarding your overall wellness, please consider leaving a review, just a line or two. I will appreciate it very much, as reviews are very important for independent authors like me.

Thank You.

Printed in Great Britain
by Amazon